DEVELOPING SUBJECT KNOWLEDGE IN DESIGN AND TECHNOLOGY:

STRUCTURES

Edited by
Gwyneth Owen-Jackson and John Myerson
at The Open University

Trentham Books
Stoke on Trent, UK and Sterling, USA

in association with

The Open University

Trentham Books Limited

Westview House
734 London Road
Oakhill
Stoke on Trent
Staffordshire
England ST4 5NP

22883 Quicksilver Drive
Sterling
VA 20166-2012
USA

First published 2001

British Library Cataloguing-in-Publication Data
A catalogue record for this book is available from the British Library

ISBN: 1 85856 246 5

Designed and typeset by Trentham Print Design Ltd., Chester and printed in Great Britain by Cromwell Press Ltd., Wiltshire.

Acknowledgements

The text is based on The Open University course T102 – Living with Technology and draws on T235 Engineering Mechanics: Solids.

We want to thank the authors of both courses for generously allowing their texts to be used.

We also want to thank Frank Banks for reading through earlier drafts and giving valuable advice.

Contents

Introduction

The aim of this text is to develop your subject knowledge in Structures.

The study of structures is about how products are constructed, so that they don't fall down, and how they support loads. Buildings, such as houses and tents, and bridges, such as the Clifton Suspension bridge, are examples of structures. Other examples include bookshelves, gliders, deck-chairs and music stands. Any of these could have been used as examples but we have focused on houses throughout the text, as these cover most of the areas referred to and will be familiar to all readers.

An understanding of how loads are carried on structures leads on to consideration of the effects of those loads on the materials from which the structures are made. In large-scale structures, while safety is obviously important, there is the need to ensure optimum use of materials to avoid waste and extra expense.

Within the book elements in the National Curriculum for Design and Technology for England are addressed, in particular the section on 'Structures' as shown in the table below:

Key Stage 3

Knowledge and understanding of structures:	
Pupils should be taught:	Covered in:
a) to recognise and use structures and how to support and reinforce them	The effects of loads: Forces Recognising structures: Bridging the gap Recognising structures: Frameworks
b) simple tests and appropriate calculations to work out the effects of loads	The effects of loads: Forces The effects of loads on materials
c) that forces of compression, tension, torsion and shear produce different effects	The effects of loads: Forces The effects of loads on materials

In addition, attention has been paid to meeting the knowledge specified as required to teach Design and Technology in *Minimum Competences for students to teach Design and Technology in secondary schools* (Design and Technology Association 1995).

Suggestions are given below as to how you may work through this book, but throughout you are seen as an active learner, engaging with the text and developing your knowledge and understanding.

Who is this book for?

This book is intended to be used as part of initial teacher training for Design and Technology, and may be used in a number of ways, for example:

- Pre-course, or at the very start of your course, you may choose to work through it all in one go
- At stages during your course (to suit your own time and needs) to satisfy subject audit requirements
- During school placement, when particular topics in Structures are being taught.

How to use this book

The book has been divided into sections which, worked through sequentially, would provide a comprehensive grounding in all aspects of structures. It may be that you already have knowledge in some of these areas so need not study them. However if you need to develop certain aspects of your knowledge or you require particular knowledge at a particular time for teaching purposes, then each section can be studied independently.

All the sections incorporate activities and questions to help you to develop a thorough understanding of the topics covered. The book has been designed for self study, but if it is possible you may wish to discuss these activities and questions with your professional tutor, school mentor or a suitable Design and Technology teacher, as this will help you to put the knowledge into an appropriate and relevant context. Answers to the questions are given at the back of the book.

This book will give you sufficient knowledge to teach Structures at Key Stage 3 level and will help you to develop confidence in delivering this area of the curriculum. There will be the time to further develop your subject knowledge whilst you are teaching.

Structures, like all areas of Design & Technology, changes and develops as new scientific discoveries are made and new materials are developed. This means that you will need to constantly keep up-dating your knowledge to ensure that you always have the latest information.

Keeping subject knowledge up-to-date is part of being an effective teacher and means you will always be at the forefront of what is happening in your area. This is an aspect of Design and Technology that makes it challenging, interesting and exciting.

If you need to develop your subject knowledge in other areas of Design and Technology you may be interested in other books in this series.

Developing subject knowledge in Design and Technology – Developing, Planning and Communicating Ideas.

Developing subject knowledge in Design and Technology – Aspects of Food Technology

Developing subject knowledge in Design and Technology – Systems and Control.

The effects of loads: forces

This section looks at the strength and stiffness of structures, through the example of one structure you will be familiar with – a house. It describes what is meant by ‘a load’ and how structures can withstand the effect of loads.

The strength and stiffness of a structure

A structure is an assembly of parts that supports loads. The parts can have all sorts of sizes and shapes, and be made from all sorts of materials. Buildings and bridges are structures, but so are aeroplanes and cars. Living organisms such as trees and our bodies are also structures in this sense. A tree must be able to carry its own weight and resist gales, and the human body has to cope with an immense variety of loads resulting from everyday activities such as walking and lifting, and from more exceptional ones, falling down the stairs or giving birth, for instance.

A structure under load is said to fail if *either* of the following two things happens:

- part of it breaks,
- part of it deforms (changes shape) too much.

A hammock, for instance, fails as a structure if its ropes snap or if they stretch too much. The structure as a whole also fails if the hammock is slung between two saplings that either bend too much or break. Another example of a structure failing by excessive deformation is what happens if you place an empty beer can upright on the floor and then stand on it; the can buckles. Similar things can happen to cars.

Fortunately, failure of houses is relatively rare because their structures are much stronger and stiffer than they need to be in order to support the loads normally put on them. So usually it is only under exceptional circumstances, such as an earthquake, that a house breaks. And although all parts of a house structure (e.g. walls, floors and roof beams) deform to some extent under load, they do not usually deform so much that the house becomes uninhabitable because of structural failure.

To counter these two possible forms of failure (breaking and excessive deformation) a structure needs two particular and distinct characteristics: strength and stiffness.

The **strength** of a structure may be defined in a number of ways. We shall use one of the more common ones, which is, the strength is the *load at which the structure fails*, either by breaking or by distorting permanently and becoming uselessly out of shape.

The **stiffness** of a structure is a measure of its *ability to withstand changing shape*, or deforming, whether by bending, twisting or stretching, under load.

Activity 1

Try bending a ruler in the two ways shown in figure 1. Which is the stiffest?

You don't need to break a ruler to prove this: experience will already have shown you the easiest way to break a piece of wood.

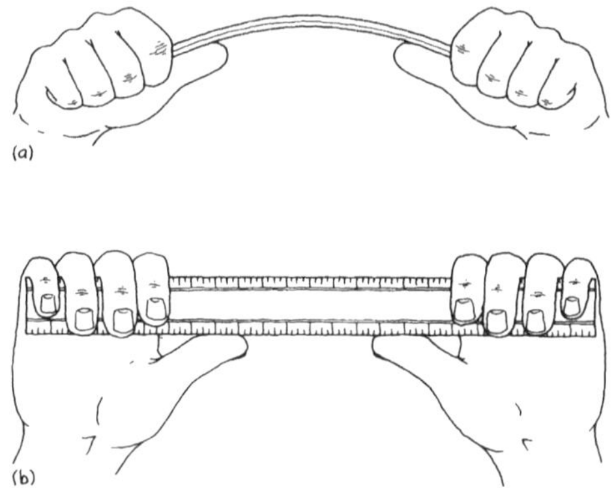

Figure 1: Bending a ruler

Notice that the ruler is much stiffer when you try to bend it in the way shown in figure 1b, and yet it is still made of the same material. The ruler is also much stronger when bent as in figure 1b.

For a given load on a structure, the stiffer it is the smaller the deformation it will undergo. The overall stiffness of a structure is the cumulative result of a number of factors, including:

- The way its parts are arranged relative to one another and to the loads on it, it is easier to flatten a cardboard box by stamping on a corner or an edge rather than on a face;

- The size and shape of the parts, a sheet of cardboard is easier to bend when flat compared to when it is folded into a 'V' shape or rolled into a tube;
- The firmness with which the parts are joined together. Repairing a torn cardboard box with sticky tape doesn't fully restore its original stiffness;
- The types of materials used for the parts, a steel box is stiffer than a cardboard one of the same size and thickness of sheet.

Later, this idea of the stiffness of a structure will be developed a little more precisely.

Activity 2

Experiment with tubes made from A4 paper or thin card. Roll or fold A4 sheets to make tubes with various cross-section shapes (rectangular, round, triangular). Support them across a gap (between two tables) and load them in the middle by hanging weights from a wire frame.

What do you notice about the relationship between shape and stiffness?

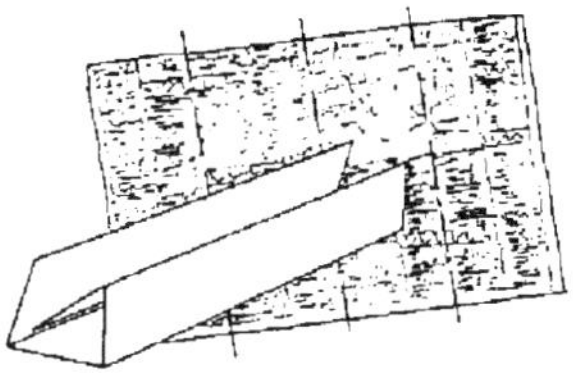

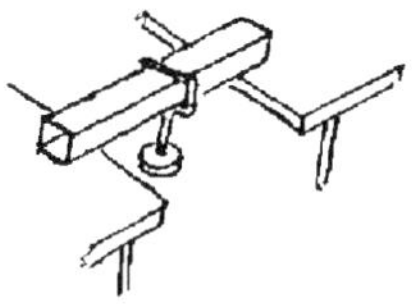

Shape of card bridge	Load carried
— *flat sheet*	
△ *triangular tube*	
□ *square tube*	
○ *round tube*	

Figure 2

You should find that the rectangular tube is the least stable and the triangular is the most stable. There may be little difference in stiffness if the tubes are all the same depth in cross-section. The stiffest should be the one with the greatest depth.

It is important to appreciate that these definitions of strength and stiffness are used to apply to a *structure* and not to the *materials* from which it is made.

In order to assess the performance of a house as a structure, a decision has to be made about how strong and how stiff it should be. These two requirements are independent. If you lived in a building with a flat roof that sagged a couple of inches when it rained, you would be uneasy, to say the least. But the fact that the roof is sagging does not necessarily mean that it is about to break; it might still be quite strong. Stiffness in a permanent building is a desirable feature, however, since it helps to prevent plaster cracking, doors jamming, windows breaking and ornaments falling off shelves. It also reassures the occupants that the building is safe.

If a structure like a house is stiff enough, then it will usually also be strong enough for the loads it has to carry. However, both criteria need to be satisfied in structural design. Your house must support its own weight all the time and resist occasionally very high winds and heavy snow falls. If it was only just strong and stiff enough to cope with all normal conditions in your particular area, then you might be somewhat concerned about what would happen in abnormal conditions, say in freak winds or storms. It is sensibly cautious to design a structure to take higher loads than those it is normally expected to support. This degree of 'over-design' is called a **factor of safety**. If say, a structure is designed to support twice its normally expected load, then its factor of safety is 2.

The factor of safety applied to buildings and bridges is normally high, partly to allow for the possibility of poor-quality materials and workmanship, as well as to cope with higher loads than normal. Many bridges, built during the eighteenth and nineteenth centuries, are now safely carrying loads many times greater than their designers envisaged. Their factor of safety must have been very high, but if an aeroplane structure were as much over-designed, it would never leave the ground because it would be too heavy. This does not mean that aeroplanes are relatively 'unsafe'; the loads they have to carry are more precisely known and carefully controlled, and so the factor of safety can be lower.

To use a factor of safety you simply take the normal maximum load to which the structure will be subjected and multiply it by the appropriate factor of safety. You then design the structure to take this higher load.

Question 1

Suppose that a small crane is to be designed to lift a maximum load of 2000 bricks at a time on and off lorries. Insurance requirements specify a factor of safety of 2. What load (number of bricks) should the crane be designed to support before failing?

The word **load** has been used a number of times because you should have some idea of what it means. But, we can't go much further just measuring a load as a number of bricks. We need to define more precisely what is meant by a *load* and the units used to measure it.

The simplest form of load is that produced by physical contact. This is the loading you feel if someone pushes against your chest. It is also the loading on a wall that you impose by leaning on it, or that you impose on the floor by standing on it. You will appreciate that a load always acts in some direction or other.

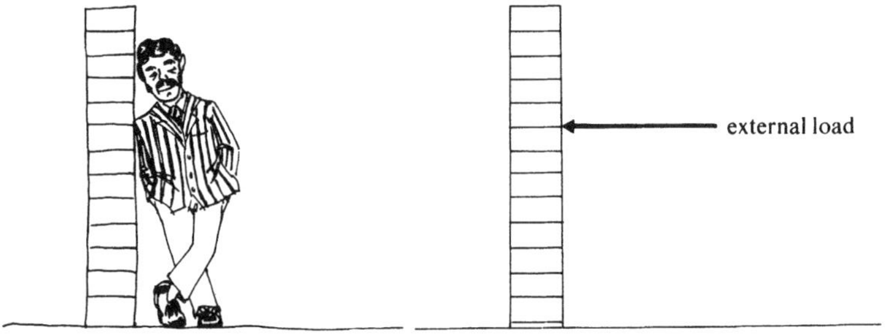

Figure 3: Diagrammatic representation of an external load

Diagrammatically, a load can be shown as an arrow pointing in the direction of the load (figure 3). This type of load is called an **external load**, because it arises from sources outside (i.e. external to) the structure.

A load can also be applied without physical contact. The type of load that you experience as a sinking feeling on a big dipper, for instance, is caused by the acceleration of your own body and is called a **body load**. You also experience a body load in a car that rounds a bend at speed. Again, a body load acts in some particular direction and it acts on all parts of a structure simultaneously. This doesn't just mean loads associated with the *human* body. All structures experience body loads, and the most common example is a structure's own weight.

You may accept this example of weight as a load quite happily without question, but underlying it are some scientific concepts that need to be explained in order for you to develop a firm understanding of the behaviour of structures; in particular, the difference between *weight* and *mass*.

We recognise physical objects as 'things' that contain matter, or substance. The amount of matter in a body is called its **mass**. Our understanding of how objects behave as structures is based on the idea (originally propounded by Newton) that all objects are attracted to one another by *gravity*. We are constantly aware of gravity in our daily lives as that which pulls everything towards the earth. When you drop a glass it is pulled out of your hand by gravity. Despite the technical prowess of athletes, gravity puts a limit on the world high-jump record and it is the reason why huge rockets are needed to put a satellite into space. The greater the mass of an object, the greater is the pull; hence the moon is held in orbit round the earth, and the earth in orbit round the sun.

In terms of understanding structures, the most important step in the argument is, the weight of an object is a measure of the gravitational attraction between its mass and the mass of the earth. The greater the mass of an object, the more it will weigh, when under the influence of a given gravitational field. In other words, the more matter an object contains the greater is the pull on it due to gravity. A bag containing 1000 identical peas will weigh twice as much as a bag containing 500 identical peas. This may seem a very obvious statement, but what you should be clear about is that weight and mass are not the same. They are measured in different units and the distinction between them is important.

One important difference is that the weight of an object, being a kind of load, acts in a particular direction, normally straight downwards towards the centre of the earth. Mass, on the other hand, is not directed – it is simply an amount of matter.

The SI unit used to measure mass is the kilogram (symbol: kg). The kilogram is not the unit of weight. The SI unit for measuring weight, and load, is called the **newton** (symbol: N). So, to say that the weight of an object, is say, one kilogram (1 kg) is not strictly correct. It would be correct to say that an object with a mass of one kilogram has a weight of 9.81 newtons (9.81 N). The factor 9.81 is determined by the strength of the earth's gravitational pull. For most purposes we can assume, that 1kg weighs about 10 N.

As it happens, one newton is about the weight of an ordinary apple. A house-brick weighs about 30 N. The newton is a small unit and you will often find kilonewtons (kN) and meganewtons (MN) used, where:

$1kN = 1{,}000N = 10^3N$

$1MN = 1{,}000{,}000N = 10^6N$

A medium-sized family car weighs about 9kN. This distinction between mass and weight, and the units used to measure them, may be confusing to you. A lot of the trouble arises because, in everyday language, people use the word 'weight' to mean two different things – weight *and* mass – which engineers and scientists find they need to distinguish between rather carefully. So, for instance, at the supermarket you may buy a bag of flour marked 1.5kg, which is referred to on the label, if at all, as the 'net weight'. However, when you buy that bag of flour you are not actually interested in the *weight* of the flour, but in the *amount,* that is, the mass, of flour and how far it will go towards feeding your household. It's only when you are carrying all your shopping home that you become concerned about the weight, as you feel it pulling down on your arms. The 1.5kg on the label is strictly speaking the mass of the flour, and the weight is about 15 newtons. If you bought this same bag of flour at a supermarket on the moon or on Mars, you would still get exactly the same amount of flour, a mass of 1.5 kg. Because of the differences in their pull of gravity, it would no longer weigh 15 N. Indeed, on the moon you should find carrying the shopping home less tiring, as it would all weigh less. This is because the gravitational pull of the moon is less than that of the earth, since the mass of the moon is less than that of the earth.

You have been introduced to the ideas that weight is a particular kind of load, a weight or load acts in some particular direction, and weights (and loads in general) are measured in newtons. Both weights and loads are examples of **forces.**

To summarise:

- the unit for measuring any kind of force is the newton;
- a force acts in some direction;
- forces may be thought of as pushing or pulling on something.

Now that we have explored the idea of a load, we can look more closely at the *stiffness* of a structure. If an external load is applied to some part of a structure, that part will be deflected to some extent, depending on the size of the load and the stiffness of the structure. The greater the load, the larger will be the deflection, the greater the stiffness, the smaller the deflection. Here

deflection is used as a measure of the extent to which a structure is deformed from its original shape. The relation between deflection, load and stiffness can be represented as a formula:

$$\text{deflection} = \frac{\text{load}}{\text{stiffness}}$$

or to put it another way:

$$\text{stiffness} = \frac{\text{load}}{\text{deflection}}$$

A common example of a load on a structure is the weight of an object that the structure has to support. The diving board in figure 4(a) is a structure and the load on it is the weight of the person standing on the end. The mass of the person is 80kg and the load is therefore a weight of approximately 800 N acting vertically downwards on the end of the diving board. Figure 4(b) shows this load of 800N deflecting the end of the diving board 100mm vertically downwards.

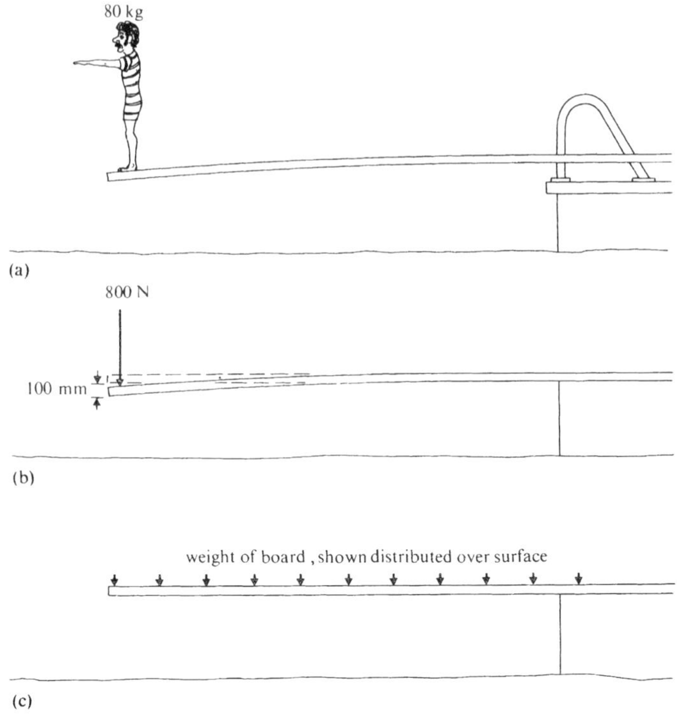

Figure 4: Diving Board

Question 2

What is the stiffness of the diving board in figure 4?

Find other examples of structures like the diving board, where the stiffness must not be too great otherwise the structure will not work as intended.

There is one further point to note about the diving board. The weight of the structure itself, that is the diving board, is a *body load.*

Each individual part of the diving board has a weight exerting a load that acts downward (figure 4c). One effect of this body load is that the diving board is already slightly bent before an external load is applied. However, this does not affect the size of the additional deflection produced by an external load, and so it does not affect the stiffness of the diving board.

Summary

- A structure is an assembly of parts that supports loads. To support loads without failing, a structure must be both strong enough and stiff enough. The strength of a structure is given by the load at which it fails, either by breaking or by deforming so much that it becomes uselessly out of shape.
- The stiffness of a structure is a measure of its ability to withstand changing its shape under load.
- Structures are designed to take higher loads than normal. The degree of over-design is called a factor of safety.
- Two kinds of loads are normally distinguished: external loads, produced by forces outside the structure, and body loads, such as the structure's own weight. Weights and loads are examples of forces.
- The SI unit of load and weight is the newton. The SI unit of mass is the kilogram. A mass of one kilogram weighs approximately ten newtons on earth.
- The deflection of a point in a structure, the load at that point and the stiffness of the structure are related by the formula:

  $$\text{deflection} = \frac{\text{load}}{\text{stiffness}}$$

External loads and internal forces

Structures are generally more complex than the diving board in the last example, where there was just one plank of wood supporting one external load. More normally, a structure will have more than one member and a complex loading. As an example, look at the wooden structure of a 15th century house[1] with a cruck frame shown in figure 5. This has many structural members: rafter, beam, cruck, collar, etc. Each of these members is loaded to a greater or lesser extent by the external loads such as wind forces, snow loads, weight of slates or thatch.

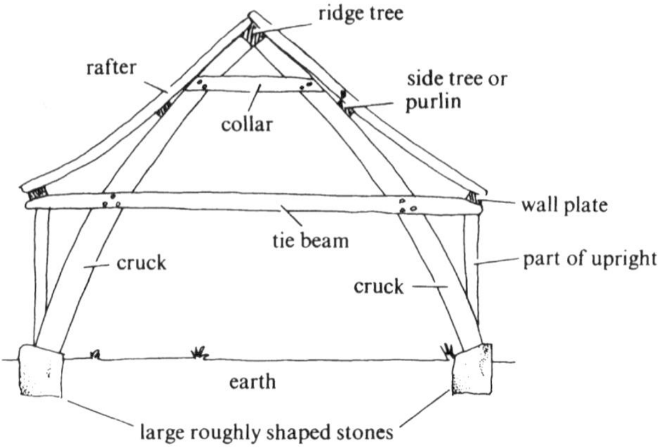

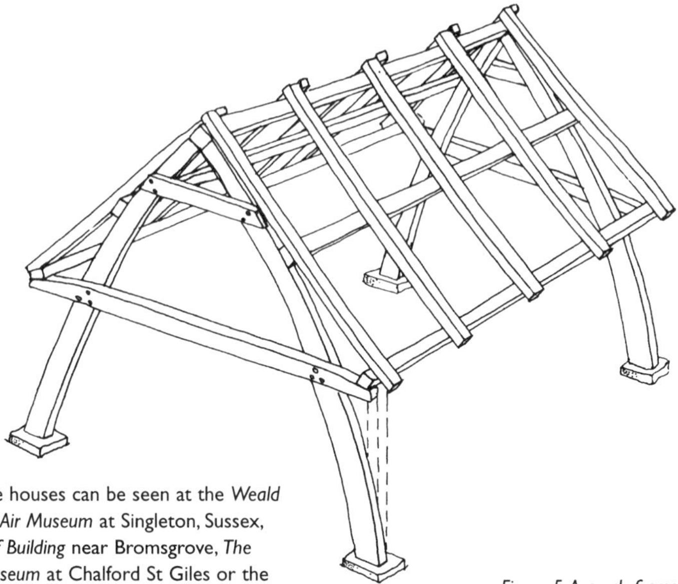

1 Examples of these houses can be seen at the *Weald and Downland Open Air Museum* at Singleton, Sussex, *Avoncroft Museum of Building* near Bromsgrove, *The Chiltern Open Air Museum* at Chalford St Giles or the *Exomusee* near Mulhouse in France.

Figure 5: A cruck frame

Simply knowing the external loads on the frame overall does not tell us what load any individual member of the structure is carrying. You might guess that some members are larger than others because they must be carrying larger loads, but how can we be sure just what load a member is carrying?

The first step in developing an understanding of how any structure 'works' is to be able to interpret how the external loads, such as snow and wind loads, give rise to **internal forces** within the structural members.

You should be able to accept that the material of the lowliest bolt in a bridge suffers from some distortion when a vehicle crosses the bridge. The internal forces within the bolt cause this distortion and indeed the bolt's only purpose is to resist these forces.

It is not an easy task to visualise an internal force within the material of a structural element such as a rafter, so we start by looking at a well-known structure, the elastic band. But first it will help to consider equilibrium.

Equilibrium simply means balance and is applied to systems of forces and loads. By definition, a static structure is in equilibrium, otherwise it would move. That is, all the forces and loads in all directions at every point in the structure are in balance. This idea of balance applies to the external loads as well as to the internal forces and gives us the key to obtaining a relationship between the two. Remember, equilibrium only means balance.[2]

One of the difficulties with the idea of internal forces is that we cannot visualise them in the same way that we can external loads. However, there are some simple ways of exploring what is going on by means of feel and observation. An example is what happens when you stretch a strip of rubber.

2 This section deals mainly with buildings, so a balance between external loads and internal forces when the components of a building are stationary with respect to each other is an appropriate concept of equilibrium. But if, for example, we were considering the forces on an aircraft, the structural forces could balance and the structural components could remain stationary with respect to each other even if the aircraft was flying at 90km h^{-1}.

Activity 3

Find an elastic band; cut it to make a strip. If you grasp each end of the strip and stretch it by pulling your hands apart, it is obviously less easy to pull your hands apart than if you weren't holding the strip. This is because the strip is resisting your pull. It sets up internal forces in opposition to your pull. If you relax your hands slightly, you will actually feel these internal forces pulling your hands back together.

Now hold your hands steady, with the strip of rubber stretched, and think about what is happening in terms of the forces involved. The 'structure' of your hands, arms, body and strip is in equilibrium; all forces are balanced. It is easy to envisage that the forces you are putting on the strip are equal in value and opposite in direction. If they were not, there would be a net force to your left or right, and your hands and the strip would move as a whole in the direction of the force.

Try it for yourself by pulling harder on one end – trying very hard not to compensate by pulling with the other hand (it is almost a subconscious reaction!). If you are not convinced, tie one end of the strip to something fairly movable (a cup, say) and try again. This balance is a condition of equilibrium: if all the loads did not balance, the 'left-over' load would move the whole structure in one direction or another. Now what is happening in the strip when you pull on it? You are exerting an external load, generated by your muscles, with each of your hands and these are exactly balanced by the internal forces set up in the rubber. Consider the forces acting at the points at which you are gripping the strip. At both points the external load is an outward pull, and an internal force balances each of these forces set up in the rubber – the pulls you feel when you let your hands relax slightly.

Now if you take your courage in both hands and pull the strip until it breaks, what happens to your hands, and why? They fly apart; they are no longer in equilibrium because when the strip breaks it cannot maintain its internal forces and your hands move outwards due to the external loads you are still applying. The bits of rubber move outwards too, and they would even if your hands didn't.

Activity 4

Fix the ends of a stretched strip of rubber (by means of drawing pins pushed into a piece of wood) and then cut the rubber strip, see figure 6(a). The bits of rubber are now under an outward pull because, when the strip is cut, they rush towards the pins, figure 6(b).

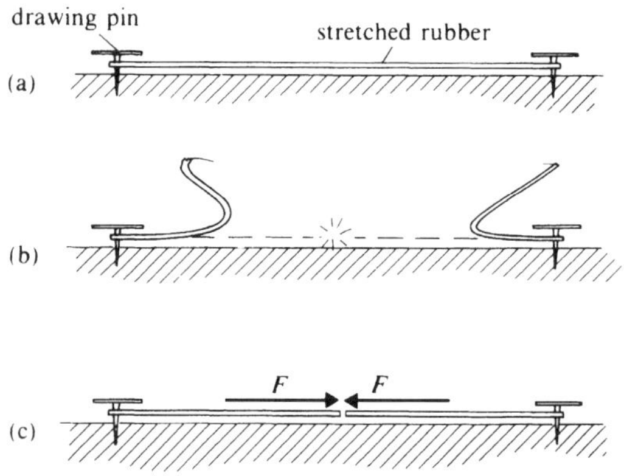

Figure 6: Stretching a piece of rubber between drawing pins

Cutting the strip releases the internal forces that were maintaining equilibrium. The effort you have to put in to pull the broken ends of the strip back together gives an idea of the direction and magnitude of the internal forces that were in the strip. Figure 6(c) shows the forces you would have to apply to bring the broken ends of the strip back together. Prior to cutting, when the strip was in equilibrium, these forces must have been present. In fact they represent the force each half of the strip exerts on the other.

Making an imaginary cut in a structural member under load and then working out the forces needed to keep the pieces together, and in equilibrium, provides a useful technique for visualising the internal forces in operation.

If we consider a small section somewhere in the rubber strip, the external forces acting on it are trying to lengthen it. The section is in **tension.** The internal forces in the small section are resisting these external forces. The neighbouring material immediately adjacent to the section supplies the external forces. If you are wondering how a material can set up internal forces, the answer lies in understanding how the minute particles called atoms – of which all matter is composed – are held together. We could envisage the section between X and Y as being as small as we care to make it. At the sub-microscopic level the tensile forces on any small section will tend to distort the atomic structure of the material itself, and it is this distortion that sets up the internal forces in the material required to balance the external loads.

Question 3

A weight of 2 N is hanging on a piece of string.

Is the string in tension or compression? What are the internal forces in the string?

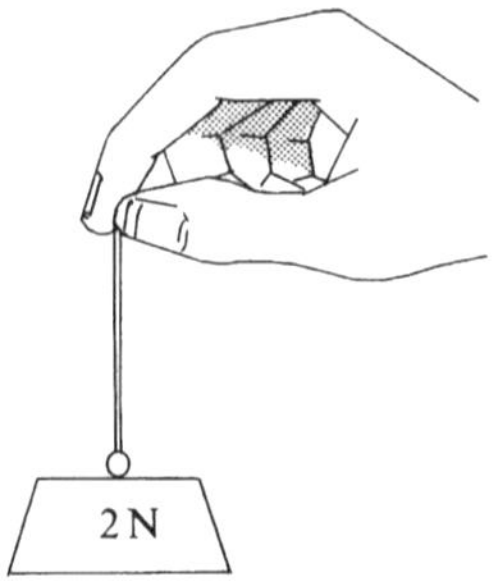

Figure 7: Weight supported by string

If a structural member were under compression, such as the column supporting a building, the forces would be reversed. Both tension and **compression** can occur together in a single structural member, for example, the joists that support the bedroom floor of a house. Figure 8 shows a joist bending under a load in a much-exaggerated form. The top surface of the joist is shortening and therefore is in compression, whereas the bottom surface is extending and therefore is in tension.

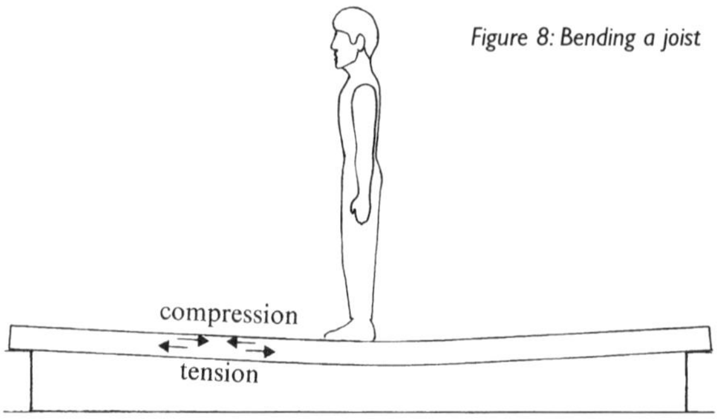

Figure 8: Bending a joist

Activity 5

Mark a length of soft foam plastic with vertical lines

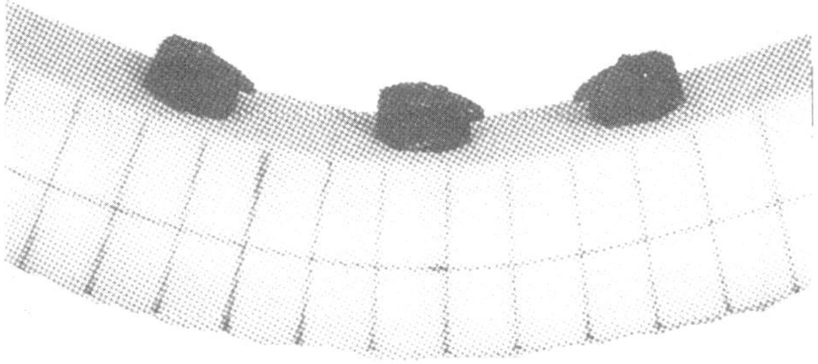

Figure 9: Block of foam plastic being bent

Bend it and observe which part of the lines get closer together and therefore are in compression.

We know that the external loads on a structure create internal forces in its various members. We can work out whether these internal forces are tensile or compressive, but how can we determine whether the individual members can support the external loads, that is, create sufficient internal force without breaking or deforming too much?

Summary

- The internal forces in a structural member can be considered by imagining a cut in it and drawing the forces required to keep the cut ends in place.
- The concept of the balance or equilibrium of forces can relate external loads on a structure to the internal forces they generate within the structural members.
- A structure in equilibrium has no net load in any direction.
- Tensile loads tend to extend or stretch a structural member. Compressive loads tend to compress or shorten a structural member.

Other forces on structures

Many structures use rivets to hold them together. Figure 10(a) shows a rivet connecting two plates in tension. A diagram of one half of the rivet shows that for equilibrium the rivet must experience a force acting *along* the cross-section (Figure 10b).

Figure 10

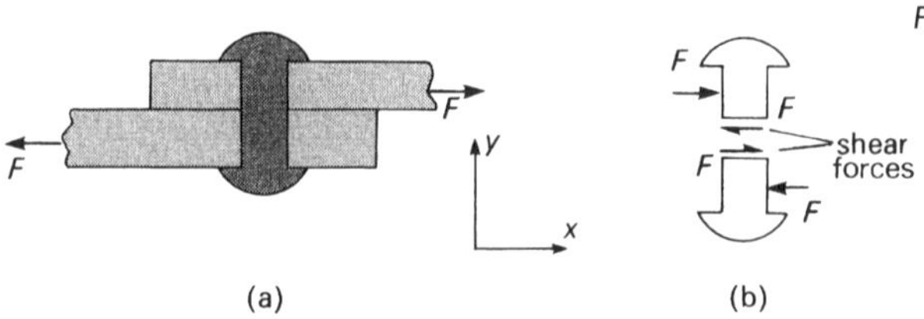

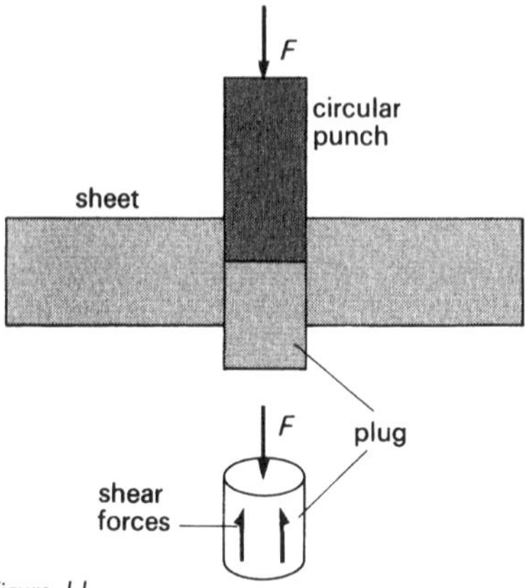

Figure 11

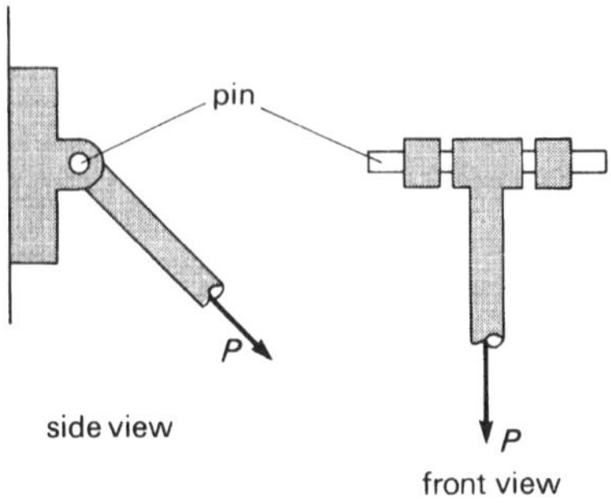

Figure 12

There is a tendency for one half of the rivet to shear off the other half. Such forces acting *along* an area, that is forces that are tangential or parallel to a plane area, are called shear forces. Other examples involving **shear forces** are a hole being made in a metal plate by a punch (figure 11), a support pin in an eye-bar attachment (figure 12) and a pair of scissors cutting material.

Shear forces are present in structures wherever two opposing forces are acting along the same line or close to it. Consider the support pier of a bridge. The weight of the bridge and the other loads it carries are acting downwards on the pier. There is also an equal and opposite reaction to the loads, otherwise the bridge would move. This causes maximum shear force at the supports. Concrete as a material is poor at resisting shear forces, as it is with tensile forces, consequently it needs reinforcement along its length.

A structural member being twisted about its own axis is called a **shaft**. Such a shaft is said to be in **torsion** (this is a twisting or turning force)and the twisting moment is called a **torque.** (This is not the same as moments applied to a beam described later in the text.) Two examples of common objects subjected to torsion are a screwdriver, and a drill bit. Naturally torsion can be applied to members of any cross-sectional shape. One of the most common uses of shafts is to transmit mechanical power; for example the typical motor car drive shaft. The longest torsion members are the tubes used for drilling for oil, which may be up to 10000m long. In other large structures the cause of twisting may be the force of the wind, such as a hurricane.

Torsion causes shear stresses acting around each section of the shaft, as the torsion forces must be in equal but opposing pairs. Working out the effect of shear force on a shaft depends on the type of material but also whether the shaft is solid or hollow. In general the larger the shaft diameter the greater the resistance to torsion forces. Making the shaft hollow serves to reduce weight, which is an additional load on the shaft (acting as a beam if it is supported at its ends).

Summary

- shear forces act along two planes which are parallel or tangential
- torsion is a twisting or turning force

The effects of loads on materials

This section again considers strength and stiffness, but this time in relation to materials used to build structures. We again use a house as an example of a structure.

The members of a structure provide internal forces to counteract any external loads; they behave like the piece of rubber you stretched, or like a spring. The greater the load that is applied, then the greater is the extension of a spring (or strip of rubber) and the greater is the counteracting internal force. So, a structure composed of various members, such as a house, can be thought of as an assembly of springs – albeit with some members being more 'springy' than others are. However, the stiffness of a structure depends on, amongst other things, the geometry and size of each member and on the material from which it is made. Let's explore each of these factors a bit further.

1. The stiffness of a structure is a measure of its ability to withstand changing shape, for example when bent, twisted or under load.
2. All materials deform to a greater or lesser extent under a load; some are more obviously 'springy' than others are. We are more used to seeing the deformation in rubber, in erasers and car tyres for example, than in, say, stone or brick. Even though you cannot see it, the bricks in a house wall do actually deform under the weight of the roof (in the same way as a tyre does under the weight of a car). Without this deformation, the wall would not be able to generate the internal forces that resist the weight of the roof. The important point here is that some materials are inherently 'stiffer' than others are.
3. What about the size of structural members? As you would expect, in a structure in which all of the members are made of the same material, those that have to support the greater loads have to be thicker than others are. They need to be stronger. For example, the roof members of the cruck frame can be visualised as collecting the loads on the roof and transmitting them to the four major supporting members, the two pairs of crucks. Thus you would naturally expect the crucks to be thicker than the roof rafters are because they are carrying more load.

In order to support loads, the materials of which a structural member is made must have adequate *strength* and *stiffness.* These are two entirely different properties of a material. To help you come to terms with them you will need to understand, two different concepts: stress and strain.

Stress and the tensile strength of a material

It was recognised a long time ago (by Galileo in fact) that when a rod of a particular material is pulled in tension it will support twice as great a load before breaking if its cross-sectional area is twice as great. However, only very much later was it appreciated that dividing the load required to break the rod by its cross-sectional area gave the same answer in each case, and that this is a significant idea – because it provides a measure of the strength of a material. The load on the rod (or member) divided by its cross-sectional area is called the **stress** in the member. One of the direct results of this idea is that when a structural member of a particular material breaks, the stress acting in it is the same irrespective of its cross-sectional area and is a measure of the strength of the material. Let's look at this idea more formally. Figure 1 represents a structural member under tension.

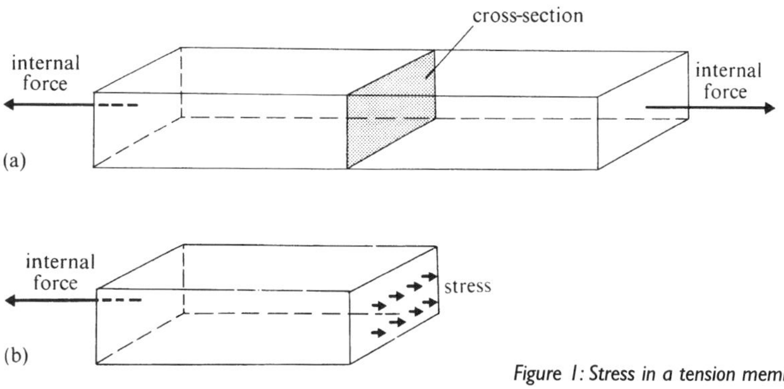

Figure 1: Stress in a tension member

Imagine a cut made through it at right angles to the tensile force to reveal a cross-section; this is the shaded area in figure 1(a). For our purposes we can suppose that the internal force is evenly spread over the whole of the cut face, so that the proportion of the internal force acting on any area of the cut face depends only on the size of the area. The force that acts on *unit area* of the cross-section is the *stress* in the member. The overall stress in the member is calculated simply by dividing the force acting on it by the cross-sectional area:

$$\text{stress} = \frac{\text{force}}{\text{area}}$$

Of course, if you want to work out the total acting force, for a known stress, the formula can be rearranged as

$$\text{force} = \text{stress} \times \text{area}$$

The **newton** is the SI unit for measuring force. The SI unit of area is the square metre (m^2). From the formula:

$$\text{stress} = \frac{\text{force}}{\text{area}}$$

The unit of stress is force, in newtons, divided by area, in square metres,

$$\frac{N}{m^2}$$

or Nm^{-2}, thus the SI unit of stress is the newton per square metre. Officially in the SI system of units, the newton per square metre is called the pascal (Pa), but in practice the pascal is not used universally, here we shall use the newton per square metre. The newton is a small force (roughly the weight of an apple), and the square metre is certainly a very large area when we are thinking of the cross-sectional areas of structural members. Very often it will be more convenient to give the value of a stress in units of, say, meganewtons per square metre (MNm^{-2}) or newtons per square millimetre ($N\ mm^{-2}$). A stress given in meganewtons per square has the same numerical value when given in newtons per square millimetre.

Where a stress results from a tensile force it is called a **tensile stress**. Similarly, a stress that results from a compressive force is called a **compressive stress**. When a value is given for a force it is usual to say that tensile forces are positive and compressive forces are negative. Similarly, therefore, tensile stresses are labelled positive and compressive stresses are labelled negative. This is what is known as a sign convention. It is really quite arbitrary which forces are called positive and, which negative, but it is important that everyone does it the same way round. You may have come across a similar idea with electrical current. Conventionally, the current runs from positive to negative, although actually the electrons move the other way!

Knowledge about stress is really important when designing for real conditions. The stiletto shoe is a problem for designers because the load imposed by the average human being is concentrated on a very small area. That is, it causes a high stress to be imposed on the floor compared with other types of shoe with larger heels. The effect is to deform the floor!

Question 1

A bar of cast iron with a square cross-section 5 mm x 5 mm is subjected to a tensile load of 1500 N. What is the value of stress in the bar?

Question 2

A baulk of timber with a square cross-section 20 mm x 20 mm is subject to a compressive force of 5kN. What is the value of stress in the timber? Express the answer in meganewtons per square metre.

Now for an important definition. The maximum tensile stress a material can support before breaking is called the **ultimate tensile strength** (UTS) of the material. Similarly, the **ultimate compressive strength** of a material is the maximum stress it can withstand under a compressive stress.

Measurements of ultimate tensile strength provide a way of comparing different materials. These measurements are made in special tensile testing machines.

Table 1 shows the approximate tensile strengths of a number of different materials. You can see that the range is very wide. It is important that you appreciate that the measurement and use of data on the ultimate tensile strength of materials is fraught with hazards.

Table 1 Approximate ultimate tensile strengths of various materials

Material	Ultimate Tensile Strength (MNm^{-2})
wood (along grain)	100
wood (across grain)	5
stone	5-30
cement and concrete	5
brick	6
glass	30-180
bone	110
nylon thread	1000
high-tensile steel wire	2000
mild steel	400
aluminium	70
copper	140

Basically, the ultimate tensile strength of a particular material is an intrinsic property of that material; hence piano wire is, generally, much stronger than, say, wood. However, when tested, different samples of ostensibly the same material may behave quite differently. The strength of a material depends not only on its history – how it's been heated and cooled during manufacture and handled subsequently, for instance – but also on the shape of the test piece and whether it contains cracks or flaws that act as incipient cracks.

If ultimate strength were the only criterion by which one judged a suitable structural material for a house, it is unlikely that one would choose stone, cement, concrete or brick. These materials are all comparatively weak in tension. However, they are very much stronger in compression and the structural design of buildings is such that stone or brick is always kept in compression.

Finally, it must be emphasised that the strength of a structure is not the same thing as the strength of a material. The strength of a *structure* is simply the *load* (force) at which it fails (by breaking or deforming too much. It is measured in newtons (N) and it varies from one structure to another (one house to another, say) depending on how big it is, what it's made from, etc. The strength of a *material* is the maximum *stress* a sample of it can withstand before breaking, it has units of force divided by area and is usually measured in newtons per square metre. In general, it is an intrinsic property of a material, but the actual value can be much lower, depending on the history and the condition of the samples tested.

Summary

- All materials provide internal forces by deforming under load.
- The internal force divided by the cross-sectional area of a structural member is known as the stress:

  $$\text{force} = \frac{\text{stress}}{\text{area}}$$

- A convenient SI unit of stress is the meganewton per square metre, or newton per square millimetre. (These units give values identical to each other.)
- Tensile forces give rise to tensile stresses and by convention are given positive values. Compressive forces give rise to compressive stresses and are conventionally negative.
- The ultimate tensile strength of a material is the maximum tensile stress it can support without breaking.

Strain and the stiffness of a material

The stiffness of a structure is an indication of how much it is able to resist deformation under load. Its overall stiffness depends on the *shape* and *geometry* of its members and on the stiffness of the *materials* from which the members are made.

Clearly, some materials are stiffer than others; some are more springy than others. You would be able to squash a rubber (eraser) quite a lot but wouldn't detect any deformation if you tried to squeeze a block of steel or glass of the same size; steel and glass are stiffer than rubber.

The stiffness and strength of a material are not the same thing. *Stiffness* is a measure of the extent to which a material resists being deformed by a load, that is, of how springy it is. *Strength* is a measure of the maximum stress the material can stand without breaking.

Just as we can compare the strengths of different materials using the idea of stress, we need a way of comparing the stiffness of different materials. In order to do this, we introduce the concept of strain.

Activity 1

Mark a wide rubber band with marks 2cm and 4cm apart, stretch it over a ruler and measure the change in length between the marks.

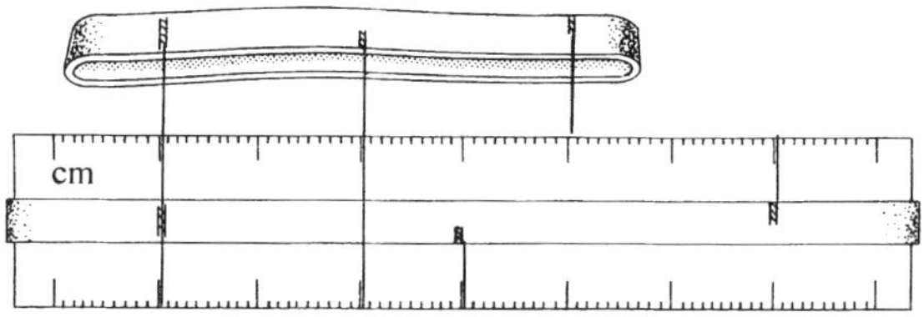

Figure 2: A stretched rubber band

You should find that the 4cm length has stretched about twice as much as the 2cm length. The rubber band has, however, been stretched uniformly along its length. Check this for yourself by putting lots of marks close together on the strip and seeing what happens when the band is stretched.

We need to specify the amount of stretch independently of the size of the specimen or the distance apart of the measuring points. This we do by dividing the change in length by the initial distance between measuring points (the original length).

The change in length divided by the original length is called the **strain**. This can be expressed as a formula:

$$\text{strain} = \frac{\text{change in length}}{\text{original length}}$$

Strain is the ratio of two lengths. Such a ratio is a pure *number*, and so strain has no units, since the units of length (mm/mm, cm/cm, m/m or whatever) cancel out in each case. However, you must be sure that both lengths *are* expressed in terms of the same units when calculating a strain. Strain is generally a small number and you will sometimes see it expressed as a percentage. A strain of 1% would be a change in length of 1 mm in an original length of 100 mm, say. In any calculations, you must be careful to convert strain given as a percentage to a decimal or fraction.

In the example of the rubber band in activity 2, if the 2cm length had stretched by 1 cm to 3cm, then the 4cm length would have stretched by 2cm to 6cm.

The strain is the same in each case:

$$\frac{\text{change in length}}{\text{original length}}$$

is: $\frac{1\text{cm}}{2\text{cm}}$, for the 2cm length,

and this is the same as

$\frac{2\text{cm}}{4\text{cm}}$, for the 4cm length.

The strain in this example can be expressed as $^1/_2$, or 0.5 or 50%.

If we agree that a change in length that shortens is negative and one that lengthens is positive, then we shall have the same sign convention for strain as for stress:

tensile strain is positive,

compressive strain is negative.

Question 3

A rod two metres long stretches one millimetre under load. What is the value of strain in the material?

You may find it useful to put strain in the same context as stress. Figure 3 is a diagram of a rod of material under a tensile load; let's call it F. Similarly, we shall call the cross-section of the rod A. Under the tensile load the rod has been stretched from its original length l_0 to a new length l_1. At this stage in its deformation, the stress in the rod is

$$\frac{\text{force}}{\text{area}} = \frac{F}{A}$$

The strain in the rod is:

$$\frac{\text{change in length}}{\text{original length}} = \frac{(l_1 - l_0)}{l_0}$$

In order to determine the stiffness of a material, we need to know how the strain produced in it varies with the stress in it. This is the topic of the next section.

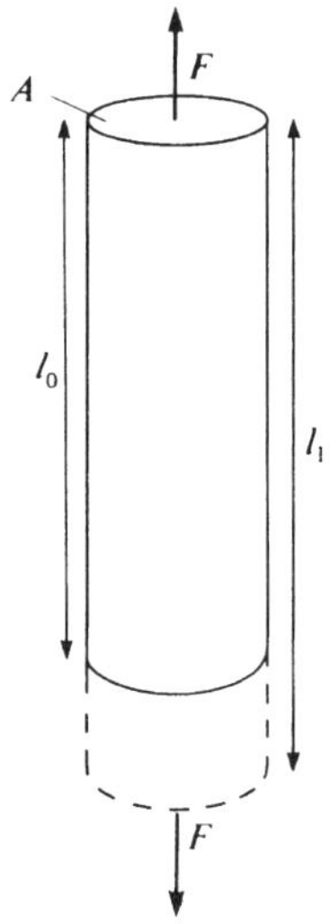

Figure 3: A rod in tension

Summary

- The strain in a material is a measure of the relative change of shape it undergoes when subjected to a load. It is independent of the size of the sample.
- strain = $\frac{\text{change in length}}{\text{original length}}$
- Strain has no units; it is simply a number, and is often expressed as a percentage.
- By convention and to match the convention used for stress, tensile strain is said to be positive and compressive strain is negative.

The stress-strain behaviour of materials

Elastic behaviour: Young's modulus

The tensile strengths of materials are measured in tensile testing machines. In fact, these machines are designed to provide a lot of useful information about the behaviour of materials under load, some of which will be revealed in this section. A photograph of such a machine is shown in figure 4.

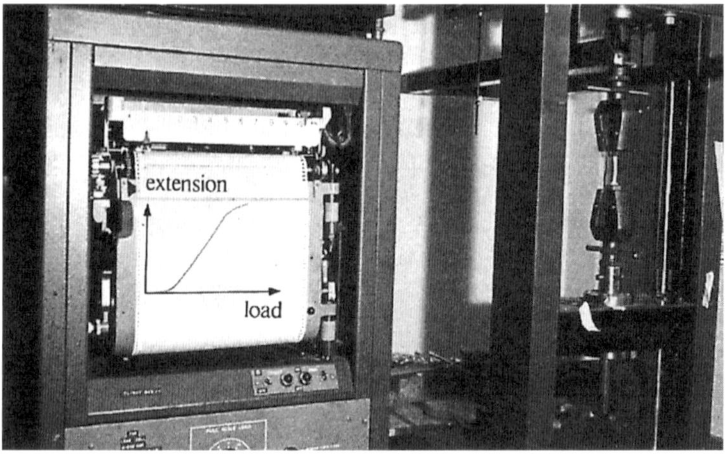

Figure 4: Part of a tensile testing machine

A tensile testing machine provides information on the extension produced in a sample (test-piece) of the material under test. As the load on it is increased, it produces a **load-extension graph** (see the example on figure 4). Knowing the dimensions of the test-piece, load can be converted to stress and extension to strain. This yields a **stress-strain diagram** (or curve as it is often called) which is an assessment of the material being tested.

Figure 5 is a sketch of a typical test-piece. The broad ends are held in the grips of the machine and the test is carried out on the long narrow part. The effects of the grips are removed because, for a given load, the stress is higher in the narrow section and so the narrow part extends rather than the broader ends.

Figure 5: A tensile test piece

When the stress-strain curve is plotted it is found that for most materials the first part is a straight line. Beyond this the curve can be more complicated, but for the moment concentrate on the initial straight portion. Brittle materials, such as (traditional) cast-iron and glass, have the simplest stress-strain relationships; a straight line up to fracture (see the graph in figure 6). Notice that the ultimate tensile strength can be read directly from the diagram.

If the stress on the test-piece is released before it breaks, the extension (and therefore the strain) relaxes and the test-piece returns to its original length. The material is behaving **elastically**, just like the strip of rubber you stretched earlier. Elastic deformation (strain) is reversible.

Now, in figure 6 you can see that the slope of the elastic region is lower for glass than it is for cast-iron. This means that for any value of stress, say S in figure 6, less strain (therefore less extension) is produced in cast-iron than in glass.

In other words, cast-iron provides more resistance to deformation than glass: cast-iron is *stiffer than glass.*

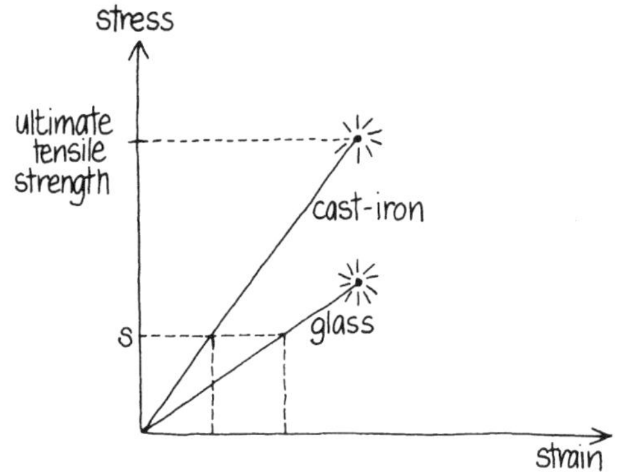

Figure 6: Sketches of the stress-strain curves for cast-iron and glass

So the slope of the elastic part of a stress-strain curve is a measure of the stiffness of a material, and this is given by the stress in the material divided by the strain that that stress produces, that is

$$\frac{\text{stress}}{\text{strain}}$$

The stiffness of a material is called thc **elastic modulus** (the word 'modulus' means measure), and there are different elastic moduli for different types of loading. In this text we are only concerned with tensile or compressive loads, and for this case the elastic modulus is called **Young's modulus**.

Since strain has no units, the units for measuring Young's modulus are the same as those for stress (meganewtons per square metre). Table 2 shows approximate values of Young's modulus for a number of materials. Again, as with tensile strength, wood and stone are very variable materials.

Table 2 Approximate Young's moduli of various materials

Material	Young's modulus (MNm^{-2})
rubber	10
wood (along grain)	10 000-15 000
chipboard	2000
stone	10 000 – 80 000
glass	70 000
bone	20 000
steel	210 000
nylon	1 500
diamond	1 200 000

Looking at the values from rubber to diamond, you can see that there is a tremendous range; it is not surprising that you cannot deform a diamond or a piece of steel in your fingers, as you can rubber. Now let's use this information.

Question 4

A material is loaded in the linear elastic region of its stress-strain graph. The tensile stress produced is 5 MNm^{-2}, which gives a tensile strain of 0.0005. What is the value of Young's modulus for this material?

In general, structural materials have a linear, elastic region of their stress-strain graphs for compression as well as for tension. The value of Young's modulus in compression can be taken as the same as that in tension.

When we know the Young's modulus of its material and the stress a structural member has to carry, we can calculate the strain and hence how much the member will deflect. For example, suppose the Young's modulus of wood is 10000 MNm^{-2} and its maximum permissible stress is 10 MNm^{-2} in compression along the grain. We can rearrange the formula

$$\text{Young's modulus} = \frac{\text{stress}}{\text{strain}}$$

to give,
$$\text{strain} = \frac{\text{stress}}{\text{Young's modulus}}$$

For wood, therefore, strain = $\frac{-10 \text{ MNm}^{-2}}{10000 \text{ MNm}^{-2}}$

= $\frac{-1}{1000}$

= -10^{-3} (no units remember)

This is the strain in wood at the maximum permissible stress. The negative sign at the front indicates that the strain is compressive.

In a length of wood of, say, 1 m we can now calculate by how much the wood will shorten. We have already used the formula:

change in length = strain x original length

In this case:

change in length = $-\ 10^{-3} \times 1$ m

= $-\ 10^{-3}$m

= – 1 mm

The change in length of the wood is 1 mm, and the minus sign indicates that the wood is shortening, under compression.

In general, deflections in timber structures are very much less than 1 mm, indicating that the normal design stresses are less than the maximum permissible stresses. This is because the structural members need to be designed against buckling. By increasing the cross-sectional area of the member to prevent buckling, the stresses are reduced. As the stresses are reduced so are the strains and hence the deflections.

The strain on a brick due to the weight of a person (800N) works out to be about one ten thousandth of a millimetre, so it isn't surprising that you can't see it! In order to see deflections in masonry you need to look at long lengths under load. Figure 7 shows a visibly bent stone column in Salisbury Cathedral.

Both stone and wood are adequately stiff when used for a house wall, which is under compression, and any deflections are not likely to be observable. Roof and floor joists, however, are subject to bending and it is much easier to produce noticeable deflections in wood by bending than it is by compression. Thus, the stiffness of joists is likely to be of direct concern to the designer of a house. In some modern houses the size of joists has been reduced to such an extent (though still structurally safe) that deflection of the bedroom floor is felt by the person walking on it and can be seen from the room below. While this will save the builder money and the floor will be more than strong enough, the reduction in stiffness is particularly undesirable when children are jumping off beds!

Figure 7: Visible bending in one of the columns supporting the tower Salisbury Cathedral

Plastic behaviour

So far we have only considered the stress-strain curves of brittle materials, such as glass and cast-iron, which behave elastically up to the stress at which they break (see figure 6). However, many materials, most metals and many types of plastics for example, undergo **plastic** as well as elastic deformation. Plastic deformation is permanent, irreversible deformation.

This is what happens when you squeeze a piece of plasticine; it doesn't return to its original shape (hence its name).

> ***Activity 2***
>
> Use a polythene bag or a metal hairgrip to demonstrate the initial elastic deformation and the subsequent additional plastic deformation of a material.
>
> Pull the object slightly and then release it; it should return to its original shape.
>
> Increase the pull and you will find that beyond a certain point you start to deform the article permanently. Can you identify which is plastic and which is elastic deformation?

Notice that when you are pulling hard enough to produce plastic deformation, on letting go the bag or grip relaxes a bit; part of the deformation is till elastic (or reversible). Plastic deformation is permanent. If you are using a plastic bag with printed lettering, the lettering will deform and will not return to its previous size.

The ability of a material to be deformed plastically is very important technologically. For example, it is one of the reasons why metals are so useful. Car bodies can be pressed to shape rather than being machined from a solid block of steel. A plumber can bend a copper pipe but couldn't do the same thing with a glass pipe, and so on.

Figure 8 illustrates the sort of stress-strain curve obtained for a material capable of plastic deformation. There is an initial linear part (OA) in which only elastic deformation occurs. As with a brittle material, value of Young's modulus can be obtained from this portion of the curve. The point A is the stress beyond which the material deforms plastically as well as elastically.

If a test-piece is loaded until the stress reaches the point B, say, in figure 8 and the load is then released, the plot of stress against strain will follow the dashed line to the point C. Notice that the line BC is parallel to OA, because

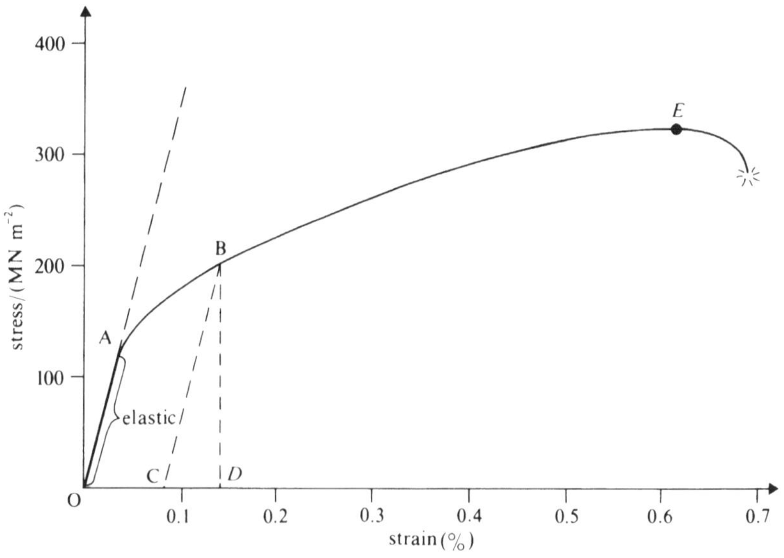

Figure 8: Tensile stress-strain curve of a material that exhibits plastic deformation

during unloading the elastic deformation in the material is recovered. So, when the stress reaches zero, the distance CD represents the amount of elastic deformation recovered. The distance OC is a measure of the plastic (permanent) deformation remaining in the material.

Two further remarks about this stress-strain curve:

1 The stress at point A, which is a measure of the stress at which plastic deformation is initiated, is called the **yield stress** of the material. It is an important quantity for materials that deform plastically – particularly metals and some plastics – when they are used for structural purposes. Clearly, structures in which such materials are components have to be designed so that the stresses on them do not exceed the yield stress, otherwise they will deform permanently and the whole structure will become distorted.

2 What is the ultimate tensile strength of the material in figure 8? Well, as you know, it is the maximum stress the material can withstand, so it is the stress at point E on the curve.

Glass and cast-iron are examples of brittle materials. On the other hand, we call some materials tough. What do we mean by brittle and tough?

Summary

- Tensile testing machines are used to obtain stress-strain curves (diagrams) of materials.
- The stress-strain curves of most materials have an initial, straight, elastic region. The slope of this elastic region is a measure of the stiffness of a material.
- The stiffness of a material is called the elastic modulus, and for tensile and compressive forces it is called Young's modulus.

  $$\text{Young's modulus} = \frac{\text{stress}}{\text{strain}}$$

- The units of Young's modulus are the same as the units of stress, meganewtons per square metre, for instance.
- Many materials deform plastically (that is, permanently) in addition to elastically. Such materials exhibit a curved region on their stress-strain curves.
- The stress at which plastic deformation starts is called the yield stress.

Brittle or tough materials?

Break a biscuit in half (not a 'flaky' biscuit, you will end up with lots of crumbs) and you will find that the two halves fit perfectly back together. This is a common characteristic of brittle materials: they show virtually no plastic (permanent) deformation before fracture. If you break a porcelain jar or a pottery mug, the pieces can be glued together to form the original shape. These are brittle materials. Other common materials that are brittle at ordinary temperatures include glass, traditional cast-iron, ceramic tiles, stone, brick and many thermoformed plastics (e.g. melamine). Brittle materials are particularly susceptible to fracture under tensile stresses, but are generally stronger in compression. This can be put to use. If you want to break a ceramic tile (or a piece of glass) to fit a shape, the technique is to scratch a line on the surface and 'bend' the tile as shown in figure 9. It should break neatly along the scratch. When you try to bend a tile like this, its top surface is being stretched in tension, and the bottom surface is being shortened in compression. The technique doesn't work if the scratch is on the compression surface.

The scratch in the surface is the key to understanding what happens. In an otherwise uniform state of tensile stress the presence of a scratch causes much higher local stress at the tip of the scratch. These high local stresses are called stress concentrations and they occur at notches, scratches, cracks and holes in materials that are otherwise subject to uniform stress. (Sharp bends or corners in an object can also be sources of stress concentration.) The sharper the defect, the greater is the stress concentration. Even if a material looks smooth, there will be minute surface defects that can act as sources of stress concentrations. The tensile stresses acting in a material are, in effect, magnified around the source of a stress concentration. As shown in figure 10(a), a tensile stress tends to open up a crack and cause it to 'grow' further into the material. A compressive stress will tend to close the crack, effectively countering its tendency to 'grow' (see figure 10b).

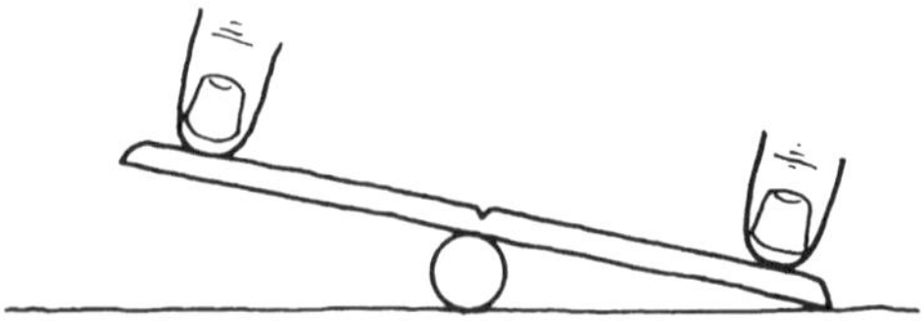

Above: Figure 9: Breaking a ceramic tile
Below: Figure 10: Opening a closing a crack

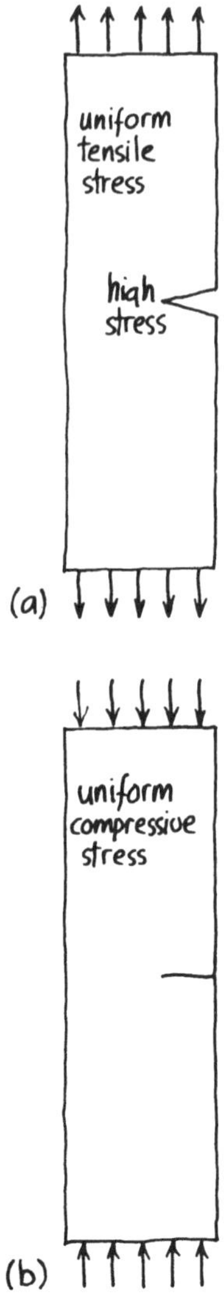

The important characteristic of brittle materials is that they do not deform plastically. The ability of a material to deform plastically makes it tough. A brittle material breaks relatively easily; a tough one does not.

Copper, for example, is a tough material, not a brittle one. A copper pipe is relatively easy to bend, but not to break. Marking a light scratch on the surface and bending it does not cause copper to break, as it does with a brittle material such as glass.

How plastic deformation makes a material tough can be explained in terms of the idea of energy. A bent ruler 'stores' the energy you put into bending it, and this stored energy is used to straighten the ruler when the load is released. If only elastic deformation occurs in the ruler, then the energy stored in it is, like the deformation, 'recoverable'. But if plastic deformation occurs, that is, the ruler bends permanently out of shape, then the energy is 'lost' or 'used up' in producing this deformation. Think of the energy that a wooden bow stores as a result of elastic deformation: this energy is available to propel the arrow. A plasticine bow wouldn't be much good.

To grow deeper into a material, a crack requires energy. In a brittle material most of the energy is available to grow the crack. But a tough material deforms plastically, and this plastic deformation uses up energy that would otherwise be available to grow the crack.

Brick and stone are brittle materials and therefore they fracture relatively easily under tensile stress. So a designer has to ensure that brick or stone walls in a building must always be kept in compression. The effect of tension is always obvious in the brick walls of a house, in the form of cracks. If a part of the foundations under a brick wall sinks, then the upward force from the earth is reduced or lost altogether and, instead of being in compression, the wall comes under tension from its own weight. This will result in cracks running through the wall. The cracks usually run between the mortar and the bricks because the bond between them is very weak. (The purpose of the mortar is simply to ensure that the compressive loads are transferred evenly from one brick course to another, evening out the irregularities of the bricks.)

However, as well as compression members (such as walls) the structure of a house also requires tension members. For instance, in floors and roofs, structural members often have to resist loads by bending, and bending causes tension on one surface and compression on the other. So for structural members such as joists, floorboards and rafters, a material has to be used that can resist tensile as well as compressive forces.

The most commonly available material which has good tensile and compressive properties is wood. A tree bends in the wind and the branches bend under their own weight and the weight of fruit, so wood must be capable of safely sustaining tensile stresses. However, if you break a piece of wood and fit the possibly fibrous pieces back together, you will notice that there is virtually no permanent deformation. So, by my previous definition, wood is a brittle material, and therefore should not be able to resist tensile forces. However, wood is certainly also a tough material: try chopping a tree down with a sledgehammer. To investigate this apparent anomaly we need to look closely at the internal

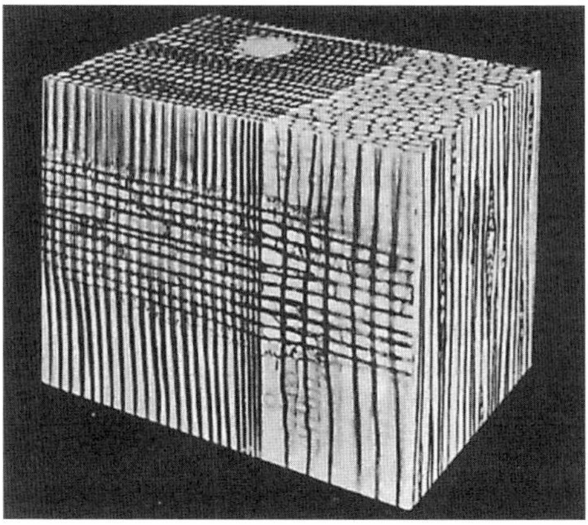

Figure 11: Grain in a small block of wood

structure of wood, for since wood is not readily susceptible to crack growth then there must be some explanation other than plastic deformation.

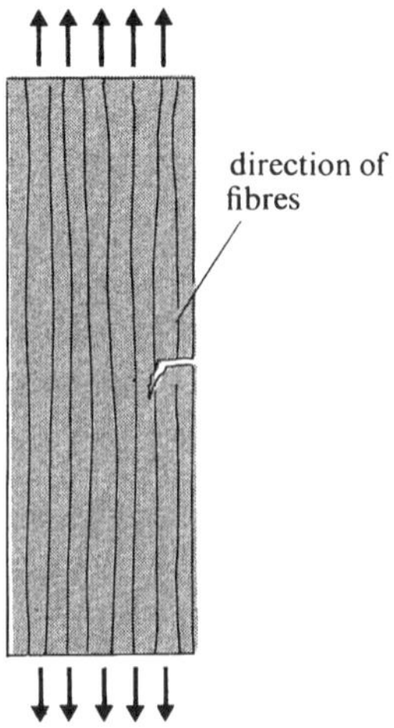

Figure 12: A diverted crack in wood

Figure 11 shows a magnified picture of the fibrous cell structure of wood, which can be seen with the naked eye as the 'grain' of the wood. Cracks that attempt to grow across the grain in the wood under tension are simply diverted along the grain (figure 12). The stresses that were opening the crack no longer do so and the crack stops growing.

From this argument you would expect wood to behave very differently when loaded along the grain compared with its behaviour when loaded across the grain. In fact the tensile strength of wood along the grain is something like twenty times that across the grain. Of course, nature ensures that the fibres are formed in the direction of the largest normal stresses. (This also applies to bone, which is similarly fibrous.) So when using wood it is sensible to copy nature (figure 13) and to ensure that the higher stresses occur along the grain, not across it.

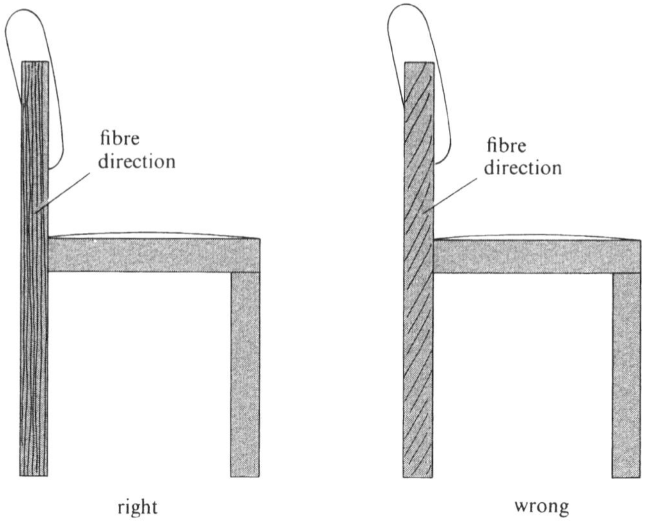

Figure 13: Direction of grain in timber structures (a chair)

Wood is by no means the only structural material that is tough but has the apparent brittle characteristic of exhibiting very little plastic deformation prior to failure. In general, such materials have crack-stopping mechanisms similar, in principle, to that utilised in wood. GRP (glass-reinforced plastic) is a relatively new and very useful material that has found a wide variety of structural uses from the bodies of various racing and family cars to sailing boats and the nose-cone of Concorde. Here the fibres of glass, which are used to reinforce the plastic, provide the crack-stopping mechanism.

This idea of making a material tougher by incorporating fibres was appreciated many centuries before science was able to explain its effects. The ancient Egyptians made mud-bricks incorporating straw, and in this country in mediaeval times the plaster for surfacing walls was reinforced with horsehair. In Victorian times perfectly serviceable chairs were made from papier-mâché (pulped paper mixed with a starch glue); the cellulose fibres in the paper are the strengthening and toughening agents.

This is a good point to look at some more modern materials that also use fibres for strength. Kevlar[3] is one of the most important artificial organic fibres. The fibres consist of long molecule chains produced from a polymer,[4] which is highly oriented with strong inter-chain bonding. Its properties include high tensile strength, high structural rigidity and high toughness. Common applications include ropes and cables, structural body parts and tyres for aircraft, panels for boats and friction products for road vehicles.

Carbon-polymer composites consist of carbon fibres either unidirectional, woven or knitted, embedded in a polymer. The polymer can be a thermosetting resin such as epoxy. Heating and stretching thin filaments of polyacrylonitrile or rayon in an inert atmosphere makes the carbon fibres. The properties include a high dimensional stability at high temperatures and high abrasion resistance. The tensile strength is of the order of 600 MNm^{-2}. The uses are similar to Kevlar and GRP.

Summary

- Brittle materials show virtually no plastic deformation before fracture. Tough materials are less easy to break. The ability to deform plastically is one way of conferring toughness.
- Cracks, holes, corners and even minor blemishes in the surface of a material are sources of stress concentration.
- Tensile stresses open a crack, tending to cause it to grow, whereas compressive stresses close a crack.

3 Kevlar is a registered trademark of the DuPont Company.
4 Polyparaphenylene terephthalamide.

- The energy used in deforming a material plastically is not available to grow a crack.
- Wood does not deform plastically but is tough by virtue of the crack-stopping abilities of the fibres.
- Other materials, like wood, that appear to be brittle in that they do not exhibit plastic deformation, can be tough due to the incorporation of fibres as crack-stoppers, e.g. horse-hair plaster, glass-reinforced plastics and carbon composites.

Failure in compression

Assuming that the designers of a building have done their job properly and that the brittle brick walls are safely in compression, what is the sort of value of total compressive load that the walls can take? To estimate this a value of the compressive stress at which brick fails is needed. The results from a compression test on a small sample of housebrick are shown in figure 14.

The curve at the start of the graph is the loading system 'settling down'; it is impossible to get the compression faces of the testing machine and the end faces of the sample to be exactly in parallel.

At point C the specimen failed explosively (it was picked up with a dustpan and brush) at a load of 80 kN (or 80000 N). The cross-sectional area of the specimen was about 500 mm^2. So, at the breaking point,

$$\text{stress} = \frac{\text{force}}{\text{area}}$$

$$= -\frac{80000\text{N}}{500\text{mm}^2}$$

$$= -160\ \text{Nmm}^{-2}$$

The compressive stress at failure was 160 Nmm^{-2}.

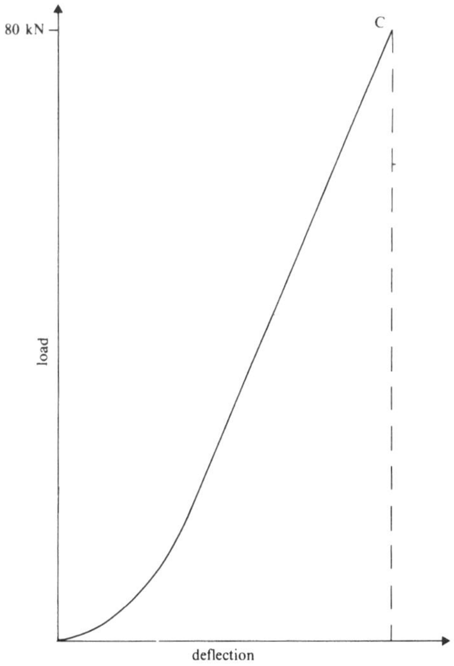

Figure 14: Compression test on a brick

This compares with the tensile strength of brick of 6 Nmm^{-2} (see Table 1); a factor of 26 greater.

The area of a horizontal cross-section of a complete brick is approximately 20 000 mm^2, so the load that would have been needed to crush the complete brick can be calculated.

Using the formula:

force = stress x area

force = -160 Nmm^{-2} x 20 000mm^2

= -3 200 000N

= -3.2 MN

This is a very high load. For instance, a single brick weighs about 30 N, so before the bottom brick in a stack of bricks failed simply from the load of bricks above it, it would need a stack of 3 200 000 divided by 30 or about 100 000 bricks on top of it. This would be a stack about 7 kilometres high. This estimate tells us that the designer of a house does not have to worry about the crushing strength of brick! The designer does, however, need to avoid tensile stresses.

Note that brick and stone are very variable materials, and the value of crushing strength also depends on the dimension of the specimen and the type of loading arrangement. So don't be surprised if you see values of crushing strength very different from the above calculation. Also, many bricks have hollows or holes in them, so the cross-sectional area is reduced.

We could use the same sort of procedure to look at wood as a structural material for the wall of a house.

The total cross-sectional area of wood required to support the weight of the roof of 100 000N is little more than 100mm x 100 mm. The crushing strength of wood, like brick, is therefore not a limiting factor in the structural design of house walls.

However, you would not use extremely thin panels of wood because the compressive load would cause the panels to bend or buckle, which is what happens when you stamp on the top of an empty beer can.

Activity 3

Obtain a plastic ruler that is initially as straight as possible. Hold the ruler vertically on a soft surface (not a polished surface as it may slip). Press down on the top of the ruler without holding it anywhere else. Try to keep the load purely compressive, that is, straight down the length of the ruler. You will find as the load increases the ruler suddenly bends.

Generally, long, thin structural members buckle at much lower compressive loads than short, fat ones. Buckling also occurs on a local scale in the fibres of wood.

If you fix the length of a structural member, such as the pole of a tent that is loaded in compression, and calculate the cross-sectional area required to support a given load, then you find you would need a larger cross-section in wood than in steel, because steel is stronger than wood, but as a result of its smaller cross-section the steel member is much more likely to buckle than the wooden member. The 7km column of bricks would buckle long before it reached a height at which oxygen masks would be needed to continue building it.

So both brick and wood look respectable contenders for the wall of a house when only the strength of the materials is considered, and they also have adequate stiffness.

However, the designer does not want to conduct basic tests on all available materials; it would be terribly inefficient. In order to assist the designer, British Standard Codes of Practice are published. These Codes of Practice include all necessary load and strength information for the designer.

Summary

- Just as sample test-pieces can be tested to determine the ultimate tensile strength of a material, so too can materials be tested to establish their ultimate compressive strengths. This testing provides data for structural design, and British Standard Codes of Practice give data for conventional design tasks.
- The compressive strength of both brick and timber are high relative to the normal loads they experience when used in a structure like a house. However, a structural member may be designed within safe limits of the crushing strength of the material but still fail by buckling. Long slender members buckle at quite low loads.

Recognising structures: bridging the gap

This section looks at some of the important elements used in building a structure, using a house as an example. It explains how some of the 'members', or parts, of a structure perform their function.

The beam

The simplest way of bridging the gap between walls to provide a roof or floor is to rest a joist on the walls. The joist is an example of a beam. 'Beam' is the old word for tree (as in hornbeam), not surprisingly, as the tree, or part of it, was the only source of such structural members.

In more modern structural parlance a beam is long compared with its cross-section and supports loads at right angles to its long axis. (See figure 1)

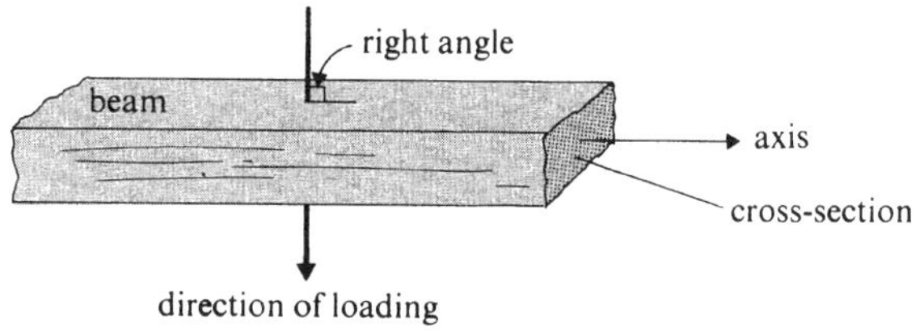

Figure 1: Direction of loading a beam

A floor joist needs to support the weight of furniture and people without deflecting too much. A roof beam must be capable of supporting loads from snow and wind plus the weight of the material that makes the roof weatherproof; tiles, felt, or whatever.

Bending a beam in one direction produces very different results compared with bending it in the other. In one case the beam (the ruler) is flexible and easy to break; in the other case the beam is stiff and it is extremely difficult to break. The joists in a house are laid on their narrower faces, so that they are deeper than they are wide, in order to take advantage of their greater stiffness in this position. Before you can understand the structural behaviour of beams, and therefore design and use them efficiently, you need to understand these underlying principles.

External and internal moments

The weight of a wall generates a force of reaction in the earth immediately beneath it. In such cases the external and internal forces act along the same line. For a beam spanning a gap the problem is not so straightforward because the loads on a beam generally act at some distance from the points at which the beam is supported.

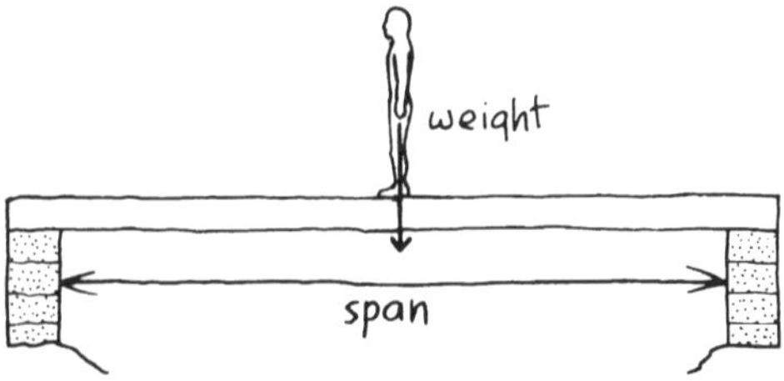

Figure 2: Standing on a floor joist

For example, imagine that you are standing in the middle of a floor above a joist (see figure 2). Your weight (and that of the beam) is balanced by an upthrust pushing down on the wall; between your feet and the walls the beam has to resist your weight by generating internal forces. The further you are from the wall, the greater is your effect on the beam, and the greater have to be the internal forces. So the internal forces in a beam are related to both the load it is carrying and the distance from where the load is applied to where the beam is supported. The product of load and distance is called a **moment**, and since a beam resists bending, the internal forces in the beam have to resist what are called **bending moments**.

The magnitude of a bending moment depends on the load and the distance between the point at which the load acts and the nearest support (half of the span in figure 2).

Let's look at a familiar example, a seesaw. With two people of the same mass and sitting the same distance from the pivot, the seesaw would be balanced (in equilibrium), as illustrated in figure 3(a). Clearly, if one person gets off, the seesaw is unbalanced and starts to rotate about the pivot, figure 3(b). This out of-balance effect is also produced if one person moves closer to, or further away from, the pivot, or

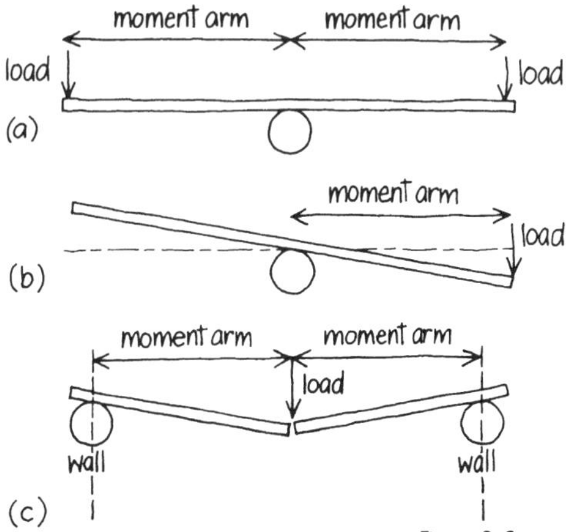

Figure 3: Seesaw

if a heavier person gets on instead. So, both the magnitudes of the load and the distance between the load and the pivot are important.

The product, load x distance from the pivot, is called the **moment** about the pivot. The distance between the load and the pivot is called the **moment arm**. So, as a formula:

moment = load x moment arm

A moment has units of Nm (load in newtons x distance in metres). A calculation will probably help to emphasise these points.

Question 1

Suppose a child of mass 25kg sits 2m from the pivot of a seesaw. How far must an adult of mass 80kg sit from the pivot on the other side to balance the seesaw? (Assume that 1 kg weighs 10N)

When you stand on a joist it bends a bit under your weight. It does not move in the same way as a seesaw but it does behave rather like two half seesaws stuck end-to-end, as in figure 3(c). A load on a beam that acts at a point away from the beam's supports produces a bending moment on the beam. If the joist broke under your weight the two pieces would tend to rotate about their pivots (the points where they are fixed into the wall), and so would you if you were stuck to one of them; if not you would be in a situation of some gravity!

So, in summary, if you stand on a floor joist the bending moment with which your weight loads the beam depends on the distance apart of the supports as well as on how heavy you are. It is not necessary here for you to be able to calculate a value of bending moment, just to recognise that it is the load multiplied by the distance over which it acts that is important when considering the loading of beams. The greater the distance (i.e. the span of the beam); the greater the bending moment.

Activity 1

1. Take a metre-rule (or metre-long strip of thin wood) and support it on two supports. Measure the span (distance between the supports).
2. Find a suitable weight, something that gives a fairly large deflection when placed on the centre of the rule.
3. With a tape measure or another ruler, measure the vertical deflection of the ruler at its centre when loaded with the weight, i.e. how far it 'sinks' in the centre.

4 Now reposition the supports bringing them closer together, so that the span is reduced. Measure the new span and measure the central deflection again (use the same load). Repeat this procedure for a few positions to get a range of results.

5 Plot a graph of central deflection against span.

What can you deduce from this graph?

You should have produced a graph that shows deflection increasing very rapidly with increasing span (the further apart the supports were). The graph is not a straight line. This means that the relation between the deflection and the span is not a simple one like that between deflection and tensile load for an elastic material, for example. In fact, if you double the span, the deflection for a given load is increased eight times; if you treble the span, the deflection increases twenty-seven times. In other words, the deflection depends on the cube of the span.

As stiffness is one of the most sensitive design criteria, this relation between span and deflection is highly significant and the designer will try to ensure that the span of joists in the house is as small as possible in order that the joists' deflections may be kept relatively small.

For a beam, such as a joist, to be stable, in equilibrium, the external bending moments produced by the weight of humans, furniture, etc. must be balanced by *internal* bending moments created within the beam. This is directly analogous to the way that external loads must be in equilibrium with the internal forces produced in a structural member under tension or compression.

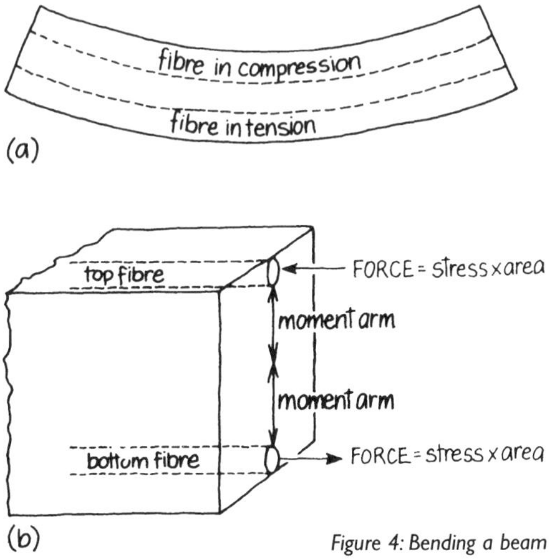

Figure 4: Bending a beam

Imagine a beam composed of a mass of thin fibres packed together and aligned along the length of the beam. Consider the fibres on the top and bottom faces of the beam as the beam is bent (figure 4a). The top fibre will be compressed elastically; the bottom fibre will be elastically stretched. These elastic strains will create internal stresses, compressive at the top and tensile at the bottom. These stresses will be related to the strains by the Young's modulus of the material (stress = Young's modulus x strain). The compressive and tensile stresses give rise to compressive and tensile forces (stress = $\frac{\text{force}}{\text{area}}$)

in the top and bottom fibres, respectively (figure 4b). In each case, the distance between the fibre and the centre of the beam is the moment arm.

The force x the moment arm

gives the internal moment. It is this internal moment in the beam that is in equilibrium with the external moment created by the loads on the beam. (External moment arm x external force = internal moment arm x internal force.)

For a beam with a symmetrical section, rectangular or circular for instance, the largest possible internal moment arm, that is, the maximum distance between the top or bottom fibre and the centre of the beam, depends on the depth of the beam. So, the greater the depth of the beam, the greater is the potential internal bending moment, and therefore the greater the external bending moment that the beam can resist. In general, the external moment arm is a very large distance compared with the depth of a beam – half of the width of an upstairs room compared with the depth of a joist, for instance. This means that bending is a very severe means of loading a material, because to resist a large external bending moment with a small available internal moment arm (depth of beam), the forces and hence stresses in the top and bottom of the beam must be correspondingly higher.

Once again, this can be illustrated by the bending of a ruler (figure 5). For a given external moment (the force you apply times the distance between your

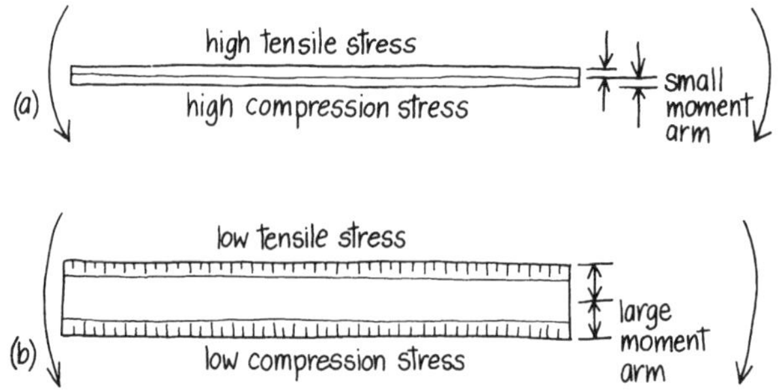

Figure 5: Stresses in a ruler

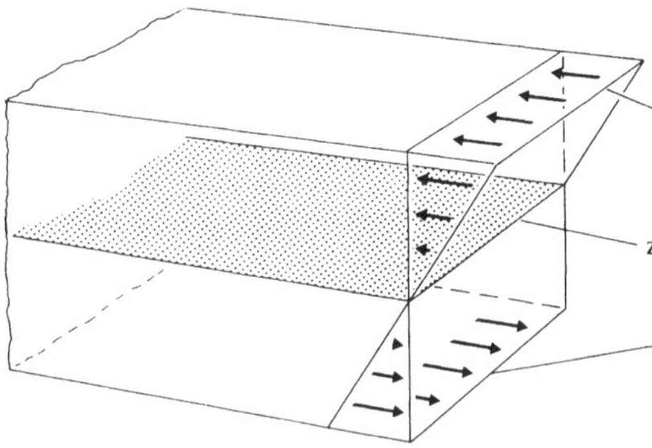

Figure 6: Making a castellated beam

grip and the centre of the ruler), there will be higher stresses in the top and bottom surfaces if you bend the ruler as shown in figure 5(a) than if you bend it as in figure 5(b). With the higher stress, the ruler deforms more and therefore deflects more.

So far we have considered only those fibres on which the effects are greatest, but most of them contribute to the total internal moment that the beam can provide. In a beam with a rectangular cross-section, such as a joist, the stress generated by an external bending moment varies linearly from a tensile stress at one surface to an equal compressive stress at the other surface.

Figure 6 shows this for one half of a beam; there would be equal and opposite stresses in the other half. At the centre there is no stress in the fibres and the stress is always greatest in the outermost fibres; the direction and length of the arrows in figure 6 indicates the direction and magnitude of the stresses. Because there is little stress at the centre portion of the beam, as long as some material is left to provide the depth of beam, by removing material from the centre portion the beam can be made lighter. This is usually achieved by cutting a smaller depth beam in a castellated form and reassembling it to leave holes (figure 7).

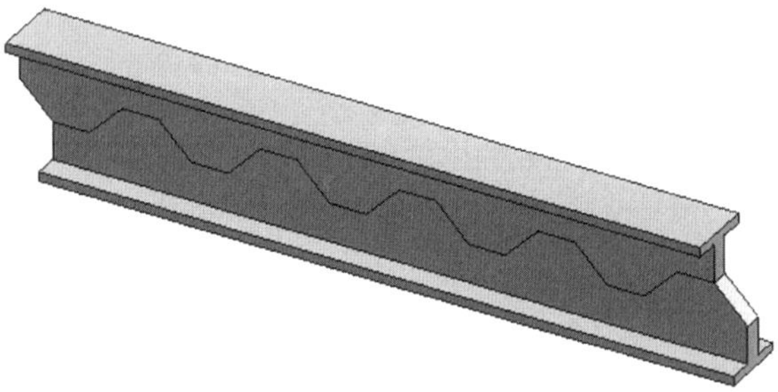

Figure 7a: Beam ready for cutting into castellated beam

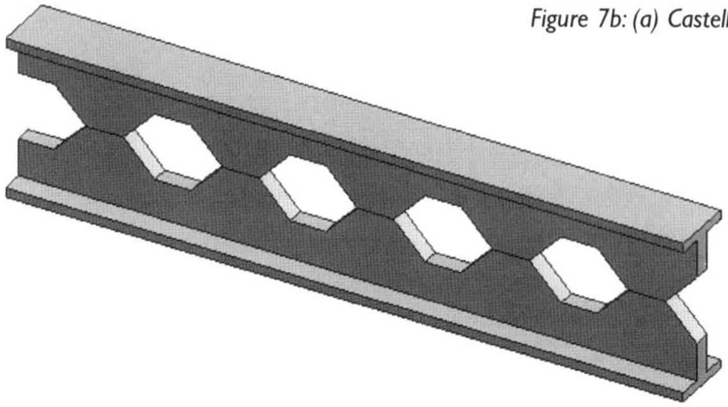

Figure 7b: (a) Castellated beam (note increased depth)

Summary

- The external bending moment acting on a beam is the product of the load times the distance between the point at which the load acts and the point at which the beam is supported. The external bending moments create internal bending moments, which are the product of the distance between imaginary 'fibres' and the centre of the beam, and the forces created by the strains produced in them.
- Since the internal moment arm in a beam is relatively small, the internal stresses produced at the top and bottom surfaces of a beam are relatively high. Beams are therefore structurally more efficient if they are laid on their narrow faces with the greater depth vertical.

The roof truss

Timber is the obvious material for the roof beams of a house as it can cope with tensile stresses due to bending. Stone is not easy to obtain in long lengths and even if it were the high tensile stresses due to bending would make it unsafe. Stone has been used for short beams, such as the stone lintels over windows. These take some of the weight of the wall above the window and transfer it to the wall at the sides of the window. As these windows are always small the span of the lintel is not very great and so the moment arm through which the loads on the lintel act is small. For the larger windows in the modern house, steel or wooden lintels are used. Figure 8 shows a relatively short and very solid-looking lintel on the Temple of Zeus at Athens, which nevertheless has cracked. Some concrete lintels can span large distances because the tensile stresses in the lintel are taken by steel reinforcing rods embedded in the concrete.

The simplest way to roof a building would seem to be to lay wooden beams across from wall to wall, forming a flat roof. A flat roof only needs to resist

Figure 8: Failure of a short lintel

vertical loads, so it simply rests on the walls (figure 9) and the walls need only supply vertical forces to keep the structure in equilibrium. The walls are therefore safely in compression and the interaction between the walls and roof is of no concern. However, flat roofs are not easy to waterproof.

It is only relatively recently that bituminized felt and the techniques for using it have become available as a waterproof covering for flat roofs. This is a lightweight material, although perhaps not ideal because of its need for relatively frequent maintenance. Waterproofing flat roofs is an age-old problem.

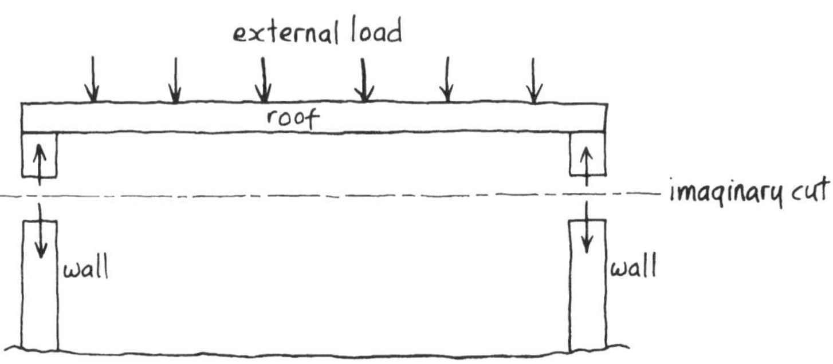

Figure 9: A flat roof in equilibrium

Concrete or slate roofing tiles have the advantages of being durable and perhaps more acceptable to the house purchaser than bituminized felt. But in order to be waterproof, tiles have to interlock on a sloping roof; the traditional pitched roof. A pitched roof can be made by putting sloping beams (i.e. rafters) up from the walls and joining the beams together where they meet at the apex of the roof. This solution, though, introduces some structural problems.

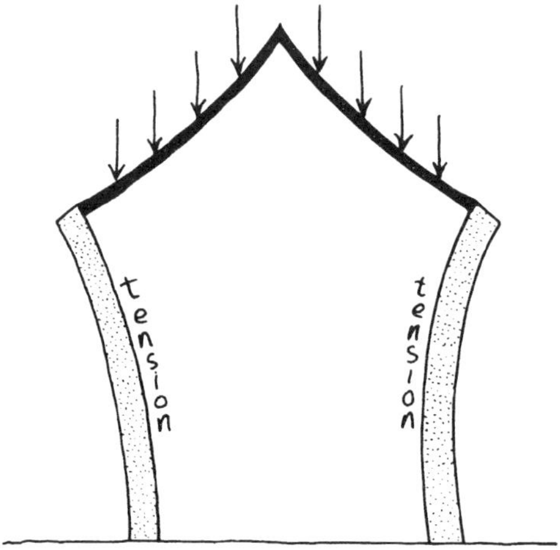

Figure 10: Bending the walls

Figure 10 illustrates the disadvantage of a simple pair of rafters nailed at the apex. The load on the rafters tends to push the walls out, causing tensile stresses on the inside surfaces of the walls. The early cathedral builders solved the problem by using flying buttresses outside the walls. The simplest method of solving this problem is to tie the ends of the rafters together with a 'tension member' (figure 11). This then forms a **roof truss** that can simply sit on top of the walls, which are now safely back in compression only. The roof truss is the triangle formed by two rafters and the tension member. It is sensible to make the tension member a beam as well (a tie-beam), as it can then be used for supporting water tanks, nailing plasterboard to, and taking the weight of someone clambering about in the loft. The major disadvantage of this member is that it prevents the roof space from being used as additional headroom to the living space below.

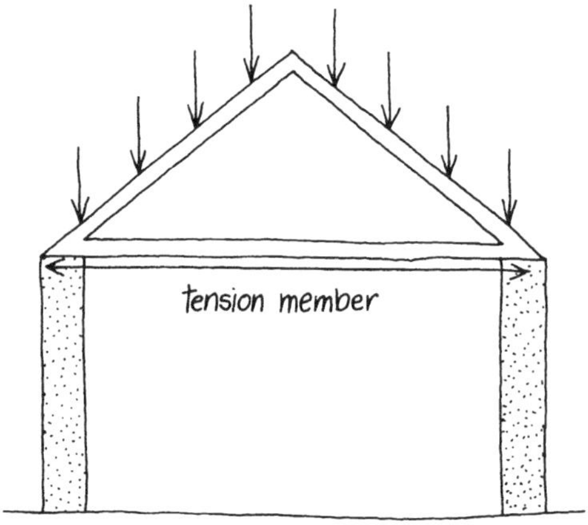

Figure 11: Roof truss

The pairs of sloping beams of the roof truss have advantages over a single flat beam spanning walls in a flat roof:

- They are shorter and therefore stiffer than a single wide-span beam.
- The inside surface of the roof space is not normally seen or covered with a brittle material such as plaster, therefore larger deflections are acceptable.
- The weight of the tiles acts along the beam, as well as at right angles to it, thus the beam resists the roof loads by compression as well as by bending.

A modern roof truss is a sophisticated and complex design. Next time you go into the loft, look at the roof truss; you should be able to understand something of its design and speculate intelligently on the structural reasons for the inclusion of other members.

Summary

- Materials that are weak in tension are not suitable for beams.
- A sloping roof has advantages of weatherproofing (and perhaps appearance) compared with a flat roof.
- However, sloping roof beams can push outwards on the supporting walls, giving rise to tensile stresses in the walls. To avoid this a tie beam is usually inserted, creating a roof truss, which only transmits vertical compressive forces to the walls.

Recognising structures: Frameworks

Many strucutres are not solid, but are parts joined together to make a strong and stable frame. This section looks at how frames can be constructed to withstand loads.

Loading frameworks

The roof truss is a simple example of a framework used to make a structure stable. In fact, unless the joints of the roof truss are pinned together (that is, able to rotate) the joint will transmit bending moments as well as direct forces. For a simple appreciation of the way frameworks operate we must assume that all joints are pinned. The result of this is that the individual members will be either in tension or compression unless, like the roof beams, they have a load along their own length.

As the triangular framework is a stable structure, it is used extensively in the place of solid material to make up large-scale structures such as electricity pylons, cranes and girder bridges. This has two advantages:

1 Frameworks are lighter than solid material;

2 A depth of beam can be achieved with less material and therefore is less expensive.

If the forces being resisted by individual members of a framework can be analysed, the type of force acting can be determined and therefore whether the member has to resist tension or compression. Some materials are better at resisting compression than tension, also members under compression have to resist the tendency to buckle .

Activity 1

From a construction kit such as Meccano, make a four-sided shape with straight pieces pin-jointed together (or use four cardboard strips with paper fasteners). If you try to push it sideways, will the shape move?

Now connect a piece of cotton or string across one diagonal of the shape. What difference has this made? How could the shape be made completely rigid?

The first shape is a mechanism with four hinges. Unless the corners are reinforced with additional pieces the shape will move sideways at the top. The diagonal string will stop movement in that direction as it is in tension. Another string across the other diagonal will make the shape rigid. The alternative is to place two strips of card or Meccano across the diagonals, but these will buckle under compression if not thick enough.

Structural members of a framework that resist tension are called ties. Those that resist compression are called **struts**. Because they are in tension, ties can be made from thinner material than struts. Optimum use of this advantage is made in the suspension bridge, typically the main supporting structure being made from high-tensile steel cables. Models of frameworks can be analysed into struts and ties by inspection or by replacing a suspected tie with a piece of flexible material, such as a piece of 'string'. Complex structures are analysed mathematically by the resolution of forces at each pin-joint. This can be done with a CAD program or in simple cases by drawing a force diagram. The external loads on the structure and their direction of action must be known.

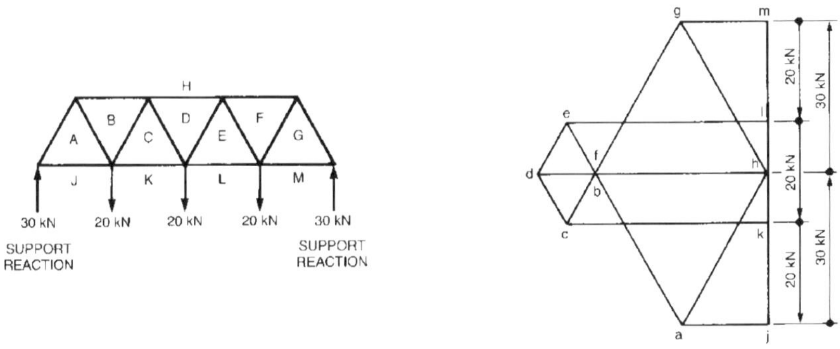

Figure 1: Analysis of a Warren girder by force diagram

Vectors, lines that represent the magnitude and direction of the forces, represent the forces on the structure in the force diagram. All the lines are drawn parallel to the members of the framework or the applied loads. In this case the applied loads are acting vertically and are drawn first. The spaces in the framework are labelled to give reference letters for the force vectors. The lengths of unknown vectors are scaled off the diagram to give the forces in each member. For example, the sloping member of the girder at the left-hand end is labelled at the support joint HA. Its corresponding force vector 'ha' is acting towards the joint and has a scale length of 34.5kN. The longest line on the diagram gives the highest load on a member. In this case it is vector 'dh' which represents a force of 46kN in the centre top horizontal member. Knowing this force and the maximum safe stress of the material, the cross-sectional area of the member can be calculated.

Bridges

If this structure is being designed as a **bridge**, there are other factors to be taken into account. The above calculation has assumed that the load on the bridge (the total of the body and external loads) is static. In a real design situation the loads on bridges are invariably moving and account must be taken not only of the highest expected load on the deck, but also of the effects of weather. The weight of snow can be considerable and the effect of wind has been the downfall of some structures. The best known of these was the Tacoma Narrows Bridge in Washington State, USA. This was a suspension bridge where the effect of wind funnelling down a gorge set up vibrations in the deck of the bridge causing it to move considerably. These vibrations were not naturally damped by the stiffness of the material and eventually the material failed catastrophically, and the bridge collapsed.

The important features of the suspension bridge are two towers to carry the main cables and a firm anchorage at either side of the span to retain the ends of the cables. The towers are like vertical cantilevers. The main load is from compressive forces from the cables. As the bridge moves, the top of the tower must move too and resist bending forces. The main cables are used to resist tensile forces as the load is suspended from them. The cables are made up of large numbers of individual cables, as it would not be possible to install the main cable in one piece. This use of towers and cables allows suspension bridges to cross the largest spans.

Reinforcing frameworks

We have already seen that making beams deeper in section can make them stiffer. In the case of materials that are poor at resisting tensile forces they can be reinforced with other materials such as steel. Frameworks are reinforced by the addition of extra members (as in activity 1). Triangular frames are stiff but rectangular frames move.

Take as an example a simple L bracket made of steel that is intended to hold up a shelf. Up to a certain load the material is fairly stiff, at least enough to hold the shelf itself. Put a few heavy items on the shelf and the metal may start to bend and eventually go past its yield point and fail. The solution is to transmit the load to the wall by making the bracket into a framework. Figure 2 shows some of the ways to do this.

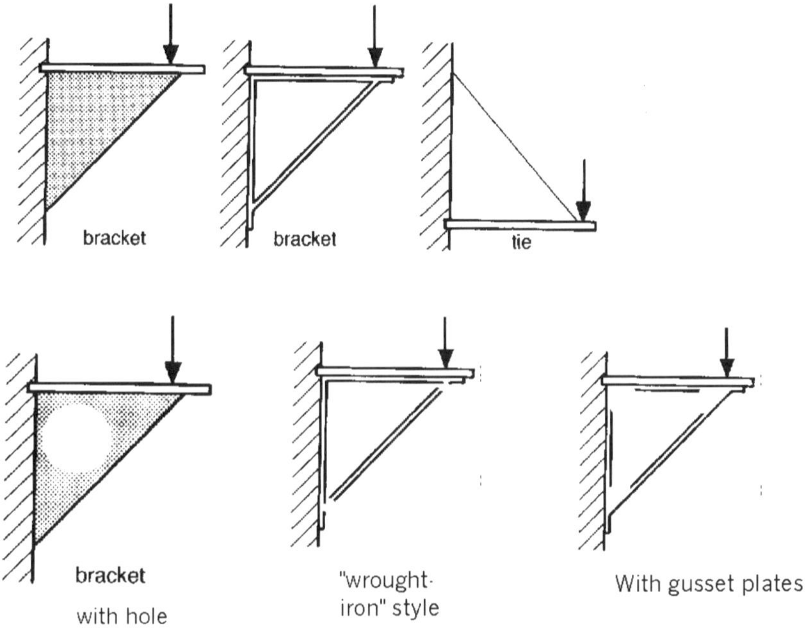

Figure 2: Ways of reinforcing a shelf bracket. Triangular plates (solid and with circular hole in), straight (and wrought iron style) strut across diagonal, tie to wall above, two ties at angles, gusset plate.

Some are more decorative than others are but the principle is the same, that of using a triangular frame. These techniques can be applied to the corners of other frameworks.

Matching shapes and loads

The method of load analysis for frameworks (see above) can be applied to any structure. Engineers have shown that the most economic structures follow closely the loading patterns on them. There are always two choices; tensile or compressive. The shapes depend mainly on the position and type of load. If the loading is uniform (even across the structure) the best shape is likely to be curved. If there are a number of fixed loading points the best structural shape will follow these positions. Figure 3 shows the idea.

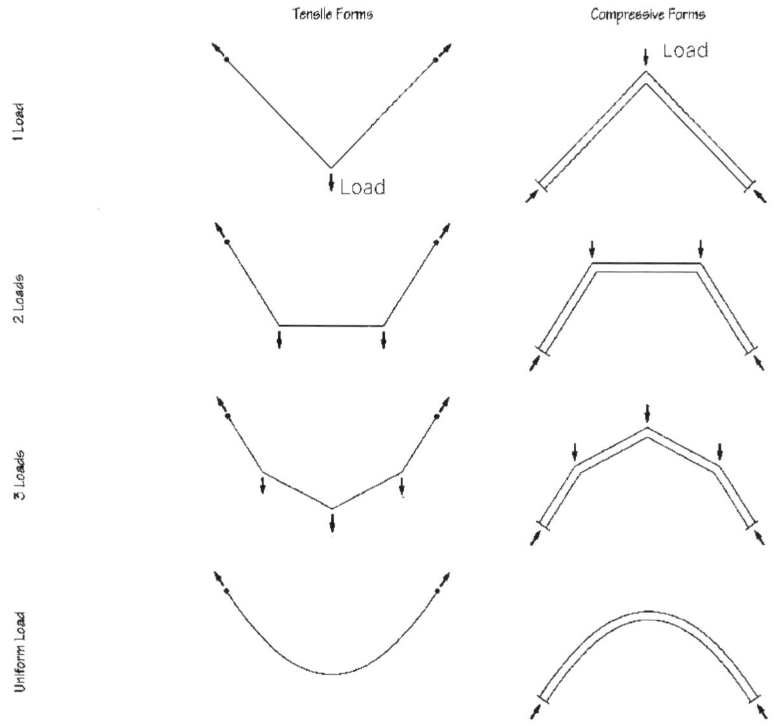

Figure 3: Common loading patterns and structural

Summary

- frames are designed so that compression and tension forces are in balance
- triangular frameworks provide a stable structure
- 'ties' are those parts of a framework structure that work by resisting tension
- 'struts' are those parts of a framework structure that work by resisting compression.

Recognising structures: in stone and concrete

This final section considers materials not generally used in house construction today, but still in evidence in older buildings and modern, large buildings.

Arches and domes

Another form of structure that has been known since prehistory and much used in Roman times is the **arch**. Typically from stone or brick, the arch makes use of materials in compression and does not require strong jointing compounds to hold it together as this is done by its own weight. The force of the load is transmitted to the abutments by the arch shape. This means that the foundations of the abutments have to be strong. They were often built onto solid rock.

An arch dam (for example, the Hoover Dam on the Colorado River, Arizona) employs the same structural principles as the arch bridge. The arch curves towards the retained body of water. This type of dam requires a narrow valley to be effective as the load of the water is carried into the rocky sidewalls of the valley.

If you imagine an arch with a circular plan, you have the basic form of vaulted ceilings used in many medieval buildings, and made big enough you have a dome. Most arches and domes have to be built on temporary woodwork (centering) until the last piece (key) is inserted to hold the whole thing together. In Florence, Italy a goldsmith named Filippo Brunelleschi decided that it was possible to build a dome without centering. By 1436 he had completed the dome of the famous cathedral by ingenious use of herringbone brickwork and stone ribs which needed no internal support.

New uses for old materials

Concrete is made from a mixture of Portland cement, water, fine and coarse aggregates, and a small amount of air. Because it can be delivered to a building site in a semi-fluid state it can be moulded to virtually any form or shape.

Concrete can be poured directly into trenches dug into the earth for foundations or, for certain types of walls, it is placed between supporting wood or metal forms, which are removed after the concrete has hardened. Alternatively, sections of a building can be cast in a factory and delivered to site for bolting together with other pieces before further concrete is used to bond them together.

For certain applications, such as the construction of swimming pools, canal linings, and curved surfaces, concrete may be sprayed under pressure. This eliminates the need for supporting wood or metal forms and permits placement of concrete in confined areas.

When concrete structural members must resist extreme tensile stresses, steel supplies the necessary strength. Steel is embedded in the concrete in the form of a mesh, or roughened or twisted bars. The steel is placed where there is greatest tensile load. An extension of this technique is to pre-stress the concrete by placing steel bars which are subsequently tightened onto the concrete to induce compressive stresses. The effect is rather like squeezing a row of books in order to pick them up.

A number of buildings around the world use these techniques with concrete. Two well-known buildings will illustrate this:

The church of Notre-Dame-du-Haut in Ronchamp, eastern France was designed in 1950 by the Swiss architect Le Corbusier. This unusual building is a synthesis of sculpture and architecture. The frame of the structure is steel and metal mesh, over which concrete was sprayed. Its flowing forms could only be realised using this technique.

Figure 1: Notre-Dame-du-Haut, Ronchamp

Figure 2: Sydney Opera House

The Sydney Opera House also has a sculptural appearance. Sitting virtually in the Harbour and overlooked by the great Sydney Harbour Bridge, the Opera House roof forms are based on orange segments. Originally the winner of an international open competition in 1957, it was a scheme that broke most of the rules and was finally completed in August 1973.

No text on structures this century can ignore the imaginative structure of the Millennium Dome in London. The Dome is 320m in diameter and 50m high at its centre – the same height as Nelson's Column. The fabric structure is

Figure 3: The Millennium Dome, London

suspended from twelve 100m high steel masts, held on a net of more than 72 km of high strength steel cables. The roof fabric is self-cleaning PTFE-coated glass fibre with a minimum life of 25 years, which can be renewed in sections if necessary.

Activity 1

Look at some local buildings to see what materials have been used and identify the structural principles involved.

Summary

- an arch structure makes use of materials in compression
- steel rods can be incorporated into concrete to increase its tensile strength

Recommended Reading

Walewski, W. and Allen, E. (1997) *Shaping Structures: Statics* John Wiley & Sons

this book has an associated website http://www.shapingstructures.com/home.html

Websites relating to structures

http://www.yesmag.bc.ca/focus/structures/structures.html	A simple science of structures
http://www.greatbuildings.com/gbc.html	World architects and their buildings
http://www.laing.com/construction/millennium.html	The Dome and other projects
http://www.argonet.co.uk/users/deano/bridges/bridg.html	Bridges
http://www.childs-ceng.demon.co.uk/	Information on bridges and calculations
http://www.maunsell.co.uk/frame.htm	Civil engineers (downloadable files)
http://www.tecquip.co.uk/products/str.htm	Teaching equipment
http://www.bsi.org.uk/education/	British Standards
http://www.csiberkeley.com/Products/Products.htm	Structural design software
http://structure.stanford.edu/	University research in structures
http://www.steadfastbridge.com/	Bridge manufacturer
http://www.baileybridge.com/	Pictures of Bailey bridges

Answers to questions

The effect of loads: forces

Question 1

The design load is calculated by multiplying the normal maximum load by the appropriate factor of safety, that is,

design load = normal maximum load x factor of safety

In this example,

Normal maximum load = 2000 bricks x factor of safety = 2

So, design load = 2000 bricks x 2
= 4000 bricks

Thus the crane should be designed to support a load equivalent to 4000 bricks.

Question 2

$$\text{Stiffness} = \frac{\text{load}}{\text{deflection}}$$

In the case of the diving board, load = 800N and deflection = 100 mm so;

$$\text{Stiffness} = \frac{800\text{N}}{100\text{mm}}$$

$$= 8\text{N/mm or } 8\text{Nmm}^{-1}$$

The stiffness of the diving board is 8 newtons per millimetre.

Other examples of structures where the stiffness must not be too great, because they need to flex, are vaulting poles, climbers' rope, rope bridge, tent.

Question 3

The string is in tension.

The string has internal forces of 2N resisting or balancing the external forces.

The effects of loads on materials

Question 1

The force in the bar is 1500 N. The area of the bar is

5 mm x 5 mm = $25mm^2$

Stress = $\frac{\text{force}}{\text{area}}$

So stress in the bar is given by: $\frac{1500N}{25mm^2}$

$= 60Nmm^{-2}$

Question 2

The compressive force in the timber is 5kN. Using the sign convention of positive for tensile forces and negative for compressive forces, this should correctly be written as -5kN.

The area of the timber cross-section is

20mm x 20mm = $400mm^2$

stress = $\frac{\text{force}}{\text{area}}$

$= \frac{-5kN}{400mm^2}$

To convert kilonewtons use 1 kN = 1,000 N.

stress = $-\frac{5000N}{400\ mm^2}$

$= -12.5Nmm^{-2}$

$= -12.5MNm^{-2}$

Question 3

$$\text{strain} = \frac{\text{original length}}{\text{change in length}}$$

The change in length is 1mm and the original length is 2m (which 2000mm to keep the units the same). So the strain is:

$$\frac{1}{2000}$$

$= 0.5 \times 10^{-3}$

$= 0.0005$

Question 4

$$\text{Young's modulus} = \frac{\text{stress}}{\text{strain}}$$

$$= \frac{5\ \text{MNm}^{-2}}{0.0005}$$

$= 10000\ \text{MNm}^{-2}$

A material similar to wood.

Recognising structures: Bridging the gap

Question 1

The child weighs 250 N and the adult 800 N.

On the child's side of the pivot:

moment = load x moment arm

$= 250\text{N} \times 2\text{m}$

$= 500\text{Nm}$

On the adult's side:

moment = 800 N x moment arm

These two moments must balance, so

$800\text{N} \times \text{moment arm} = 500\text{Nm}$

$$\text{moment arm} = \frac{500\text{Nm}}{800\text{N}}$$

$= 0.625\text{m}$

DEVELOPING SUBJECT KNOWLEDGE IN DESIGN AND TECHNOLOGY:

STRUCTURES